Say It Right in

SPANISH

**Easily Pronounced
Language Systems, Inc.**

Clyde Peters, Author

New York   Chicago   San Francisco   Lisbon   London   Madrid   Mexico City
Milan   New Delhi   San Juan   Seoul   Singapore   Sydney   Toronto

Library of Congress Cataloging-in-Publication Data

Say it right in Spanish / by Easily Pronounced Language Systems.
      p.   cm. — (Say it right)
     "Infinite destinations, one pronunciation system."
     Includes index.
     ISBN 0-07-146918-4 (alk. paper)
     1. Spanish language—Pronunciation.   I. Easily Pronounced Language
Systems.   II. Series.

   PC4137.S28   2006
   468.3'421—dc22   2005058359

8 9 10 11 12 13 14 15 16 17 18 19 20 21 22 23 24   FGR/FGR 0 9

ISBN 978-0-07-146918-0
MHID   0-07-146918-4

McGraw-Hill books are available at special quantity discounts to use as premiums and sales promotions or for use in corporate training programs. To contact a representative, please visit the Contact Us pages at www.mhprofessional.com.

Also available: *Say It Right in Arabic* • *Say It Right in Brazilian Portuguese* • *Say It Right in Chinese* • *Say It Right in Chinese, Audio Edition* • *Say It Right in French* • *Say It Right in French, Audio Edition* • *Say It Right in German* • *Say It Right in Italian* • *Say It Right in Italian, Audio Edition* • *Say It Right in Japanese* • *Say It Right in Korean* • *Say It Right in Russian* • *Say It Right in Spanish, Audio Edition* • *Dígalo correctamente en inglés [Say It Right in English]*

Author: Clyde Peters
Illustrations: Luc Nisset

Acknowledgments

President, EPLS Corporation: Betty Chapman, www.isayitright.com
Priscilla Leal Bailey, Senior Series Editor
Francisco J. Madrigal, Spanish Language Consultant

This book is printed on acid-free paper.

CONTENTS

INTRODUCTION

The SAY IT RIGHT FOREIGN LANGUAGE PHRASE BOOK SERIES has been developed with the conviction that learning to speak a foreign language should be fun and easy!

All SAY IT RIGHT phrase books feature the EPLS Vowel Symbol System, a revolutionary phonetic system that stresses consistency, clarity, and above all, simplicity!

Since this unique phonetic system is used in all SAY IT RIGHT phrase books, you only have to learn the VOWEL SYMBOL SYSTEM ONCE!

The SAY IT RIGHT series uses the easiest phrases possible for English speakers to pronounce and is designed to reflect how foreign languages are used by native speakers.

You will be amazed at how confidence in your pronunciation leads to an eagerness to talk to other people in their own language.

Whether you want to learn a new language for travel, education, business, study, or personal enrichment, SAY IT RIGHT phrase books offer a simple and effective method of pronunciation and communication.

PRONUNCIATION GUIDE

Most English speakers are familiar with the Spanish word **Taco**. This is how the correct pronunciation is represented in the EPLS Vowel Symbol System.

All Spanish vowel sounds are assigned a specific non-changing symbol. When these symbols are used in conjunction with consonants and read normally, pronunciation of even the most difficult foreign word becomes incredibly EASY.

On the following page are all the EPLS Vowel Symbols used in this book. They are EASY to LEARN since their sounds are familiar. Beneath each symbol are three English words which contain the sound of the symbol.

Practice pronouncing the words under each symbol until you mentally associate the correct vowel sound with the correct symbol. Most symbols are pronounced the way they look!

THE SAME BASIC SYMBOLS ARE USED IN ALL SAY IT RIGHT PHRASE BOOKS!

EPLS VOWEL SYMBOL SYSTEM

Ⓐ

Ace
Bake
Safe

ⒺⒺ

See
Feet
Meet

Ⓘ

Ice
Kite
Pie

Ⓞ

Oak
Cold
Sold

ⓄⓄ

Cool
Pool
Too

ⓔ

Men
Red
Bed

ⓐⓗ

Mom
Hot
Off

ⓞⓨ

Toy
Boy
Joy

ⓞⓦ

Cow
How
Now

EPLS CONSONANTS

Consonants are letters like **T**, **D**, and **K**. They are easy to recognize and their pronunciation seldom changes. The following EPLS pronunciation guide letters represent some unique Spanish consonant sounds.

ß   Represents a rolled **r** sound.

ß̰   Represents a longer rolled **r** sound.

V   Represents the Spanish letter **v** and is pronounced like the **v** in vine but very softly. Depending on your location you will often hear the Spanish **v** pronounced like the **b** in **b**oy.

B   Represents the Spanish letter **b** and sounds like the **b** in **b**oy. Sometimes, the Spanish **b** is pronounced so softly that the lips barely touch. You must listen closely to a native speaker to master this sound.

PRONUNCIATION TIPS

- Each pronunciation guide word is broken into syllables. Read each word slowly, one syllable at a time, increasing speed as you become more familiar with the system.

- In Spanish it is important to emphasize certain syllables. This mark (´) over the syllable reminds you to stress that syllable.

- It is estimated that nearly 300 million people now speak Spanish around the world. Don't be surprised to hear variations in the meanings and pronunciation of some Spanish words. To perfect your Spanish accent you must listen closely to Spanish speakers and adjust your speech accordingly.

- The pronunciation and word choices in this book were chosen for their simplicity and effectiveness.

- In northern Spain, **z** before any letter and **c** before **e** or **i** are pronounced like the **th** in **th**in. In southern Spain and most of Latin America, **z** by itself and **c** before **e** or **i** sound like an **s**. In this phrase book the **s** sound is used for **z** and **c** because of its wider usage throughout the Spanish-speaking world.

- **PFV** is an abbreviation for **por favor** which means "please" in Spanish. You will see it used throughout the book.

ICONS USED IN THIS BOOK

KEY WORDS

You will find this icon at the beginning of chapters indicating key words relating to chapter content. These are important words to become familiar with.

PHRASEMAKER

The Phrasemaker icon provides the traveler with a choice of phrases that allows the user to make his or her own sentences.

Say It
Right in
SPANISH

ESSENTIAL WORDS AND PHRASES

Here are some basic words and phrases that will help you express your needs and feelings in Spanish.

Hello

Hola

OÓ-L ah

How are you?

¿Cómo está?

KOÓ-MO ēS-Tahʹ

Fine / Very well

Muy bien

MWEE BEE-ēN

And you?

¿Y usted?

EE OOS-TēʹD

Good-bye

Adiós

ah-DEE-OÓS

Good morning

Buenos días

BWĕ-NOS DĒ-ahS

Good evening / Good afternoon

Buenas tardes

BWĕ-NahS TahR-DĕS

Good night

Buenas noches

BWĕ-NahS NO-CHĕS

Mr.

Señor

SĕN-YOR

Mrs.

Señora

SĕN-YO-Rah

Miss

Señorita

SĕN-YO-RĒ-Tah

Yes

Sí

S**EE**

No

No

N**O**

Please

Por favor

P**O**R F**ah**-V**O**R

Abbreviated PFV throughout book

Thank you

Gracias

GR**ah**-S**EE**-**ah**S

Excuse me

Perdón   Con permiso

P**e**R-D**O**N   K**O**N P**e**R-M**EE**-S**O**

I'm sorry

Lo siento   Perdón

L**O** S**EE**-**e**N-T**O**   P**e**R-D**O**N

I am a tourist.

Soy turista.

Soy TOO-REES-Tah

I do not speak Spanish.

No hablo español.

NO ah-BLO eS-Pahn-YOL

I speak a little Spanish.

Hablo un poco de español.

ah-BLO oon PO-KO De eS-Pahn-YOL

Do you understand English?

¿Entiende inglés?

eN-TEE-eN-De eN-GLeS

I don't understand!

¡No entiendo!

NO eN-TEE-eN-DO

Please repeat.

Repita, por favor.

Re-PEE-Tah POR Fah-VOR

More slowly, please.

Más despacio, por favor.

MahS DeS-Pah-SEE-O PFV

FEELINGS

I want...

Quiero...

KEE-ê-RO

I have...

Tengo...

TêN-GO...

I know.

Yo sé.

YO Sê

I don't know.

No sé.

NO Sê

I like it.

Me gusta.

Mê GOOS-Tah

I don't like it.

No me gusta.

NO Mê GOOS-Tah

I'm lost.

Estoy perdido. (male)   Estoy perdida. (female)

ⓔS-Tⓞⓨ́ Pⓔ́R-Dⓔⓔ́-Dⓞ (Dⓐⓗ)

I'm in a hurry.

Tengo prisa.

Tⓔ́N-Gⓞ PRⓔⓔ́-Sⓐⓗ

I'm tired.

Estoy cansado. (male) Estoy cansada. (female)

ⓔS-Tⓞⓨ́ KⓐⓗN-Sⓐⓗ́-Dⓞ (ⓐⓗ)

I'm ill.

Estoy enfermo. (male) Estoy enferma. (female)

ⓔS-Tⓞⓨ́ ⓔN-Fⓔ́R-Mⓞ (ⓐⓗ)

I'm hungry.

Tengo hambre.

Tⓔ́N-Gⓞ ⓐⓗ́M-BRⓔ

I'm thirsty.

Tengo sed.

Tⓔ́N-Gⓞ Sⓔ́D

I'm angry.

Estoy enojado. (male)   Estoy enojada. (female)

ⓔ́S-Tⓞⓨ́ ⓔ́N-Ⓞ-Hⓐⓗ́-Dⓞ (ⓐⓗ)

INTRODUCTIONS

My name is...

Me llamo...

Mӗ Yah-MO...

What's your name?

¿Cómo se llama usted?

KO-MO Sӗ Yah-Mah ooS-TӗD

Where are you from?

¿De dónde es usted?

Dӗ DON-Dӗ ӗS ooS-TӗD

Do you live here?

¿Vive usted aquí?

VEE-Vӗ ooS-TӗD ah-KEE

I just arrived.

Acabo de llegar.

ah-Kah-BO Dӗ Yӗ-Gah R

What hotel are you [staying] at?

¿En qué hotel está usted?

ӗN Kӗ O-TӗL ӗS-Tah ooS-TӗD

I'm at the...hotel.

Estoy en el hotel...

ⓔS-Tⓞⓨ́ ⓔN ⓔL ⓞ-TⓔĹ

It was nice to meet you.

Mucho gusto.

Mⓞⓞ́-CHⓞ Gⓞⓞ́S-Tⓞ

The pronunciation guide G is pronounced like the **g** in **g**o.

See you later.

Hasta luego.

ⓐⓗ́S-Tⓐⓗ Lⓞⓞ-ⓐ́-Gⓞ

See you next time.

Hasta la vista.

ⓐⓗ́S-Tⓐⓗ Lⓐⓗ VⓔⒺ-STⓤⓗ

Good luck!

¡Buena suerte!

BWⓔ́-Nⓐⓗ SWⓔ́R̃-Tⓔ

You will notice that in Spanish spelling, the letter **e** is sometimes pronounced like the **e** in r**e**d and sometimes like the **a** in c**a**ke. This will vary from region to region and will not affect the understanding of the word.

THE BIG QUESTIONS

Who?

¿Quién?

KĒ-ĒN

Who is it?

¿Quién es?

KĒ-ĒN ĒS

What?

¿Qué?   ¿Cómo?

KĒ KŌ-MŌ

Use **¿cómo?** if you didn't hear well or want something repeated.

What's that?

¿Qué es eso?

KĒ ĒS Ē-SŌ

When?

¿Cuándo?

KWahN-DŌ

Where?

¿Dónde?

DŌN-DĒ

Where is...?

¿Dónde está...?

DON-De eS-Tah...

Which?

¿Cuál?

KWahL

Why?

¿Por qué?

POB Ke

How?

¿Cómo?

KO-MO

How much? (does it cost)

¿Cuánto?

KWahN-TO

KW sounds like the qu in quit.

How long?

¿Cuánto tiempo?

KWahN-TO Tee-eMPO

ASKING FOR THINGS

The following phrases are valuable for directions, food, help, etc.

I would like...

Quisiera...

K**EE**-S**EE**-**ē**-R**ah**...

I need...

Necesito...

N**ē**-S**ē**-S**EE**-T**O**...

Can you...

Puede usted...

PW**ē**-D**ē** **oo**S-T**ē**D...

When asking for things be sure to say <u>please</u> and <u>thank you</u>.

Please	**Thank you**
Por Favor	Gracias
P**O**R F**ah**-V**O**R	GR**ah**-S**EE**-**ah**S

PHRASEMAKER

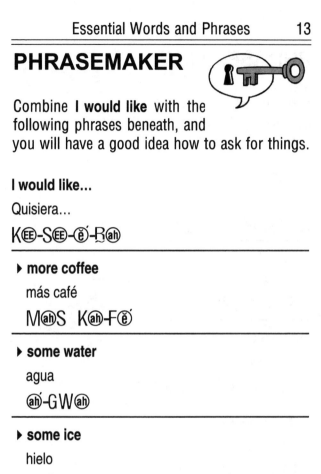

Combine **I would like** with the
following phrases beneath, and
you will have a good idea how to ask for things.

I would like...

Quisiera...

KEE-SEE-ĕ́-Rah

▸ **more coffee**

más café

MahS Kah-Fĕ́

▸ **some water**

agua

áh-GWah

▸ **some ice**

hielo

Yĕ́-LO

▸ **the menu**

la carta

Lah KáhR-Tah

PHRASEMAKER

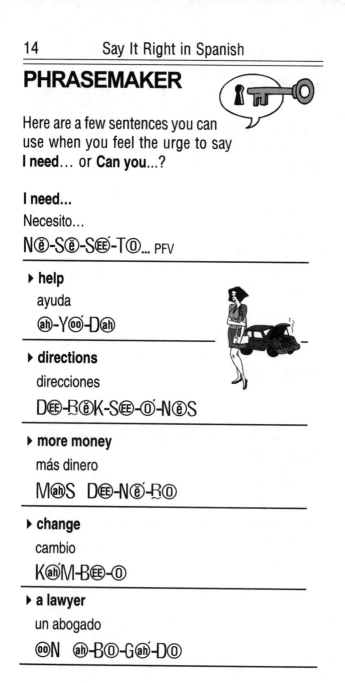

Here are a few sentences you can use when you feel the urge to say **I need**… or **Can you**...?

I need...
Necesito…
Nⓔ-Sⓔ-SEE-TⓄ… PFV

▶ **help**
ayuda
ⓐⓗ-Yⓞⓞ-Dⓐⓗ

▶ **directions**
direcciones
DEE-RⓔⓒK-SEE-Ⓞ-Nⓔ S

▶ **more money**
más dinero
Mⓐⓗ S   DEE-Nⓔⓗ-RⓄ

▶ **change**
cambio
Kⓐⓗ M-BEE-Ⓞ

▶ **a lawyer**
un abogado
ⓞⓞN   ⓐⓗ-BⓄ-Gⓐⓗ-DⓄ

PHRASEMAKER

Can you...

¿Puede usted…

PWĕ-Dĕ ooS-TĕD…

▸ **help me?**

ayudarme?

ah-Yoo-Dah'R-Mĕ

▸ **show me?**

enseñarme?

ĕN-SĕN-Yah'R-Mĕ

▸ **give me...?**

darme…?

Dah'R-Mĕ…

▸ **tell me...?**

decirme…?

Dĕ-SEE'R-Mĕ

▸ **take me to...?**

llevarme al…?

Yĕ'-Vah'R-Mĕ ah'L…

ASKING THE WAY

No matter how independent you are, sooner or later you'll probably have to ask for directions.

Where is...?

¿Dónde está...?

DŌN-Dĕ ĕS-Tah...

Is it near?

¿Está cerca?

ĕS-Tah SĕR-Kah

Is it far?

¿Está lejos?

ĕS-Tah Lĕ-HOS

I'm lost!

¡Estoy perdido! (male) Estoy perdida! (female)

ĕS-Toy PĕR-Dĕĕ-DO (Dah)

I'm looking for...

Estoy buscando...

ĕS-Toy BōōS-KahN-DO...

PHRASEMAKER

Where is...

¿Dónde está...

DON-De eS-Tah...

▶ **the restroom?**

el baño?

eL Bahn-Yo

▶ **the telephone?**

el teléfono?

eL Te-Le-Fo-No

▶ **the beach?**

la playa?

Lah PLah-Yah

▶ **the hotel...?**

el hotel...?

eL O-TeL...

▶ **the train for...?**

el tren para...?

eL TReN Pah-Rah...

TIME

What time is it?

¿Qué hora es?

K(ĕ)   (Ō)-R(ah)   (ĕ)S

Morning

La mañana

L(ah)   M(ah)N-Y(ah)-N(ah)

Noon

El mediodía

(ĕ)L   M(ĕ)-D(EE)-(O)-D(EE)-(ah)

Night

La noche

L(ah)   N(Ō)-CH(ĕ)

Today

Hoy

(oy)

In Spanish spelling the **h** is always silent.

Tomorrow

Mañana

M(ah)N-Y(ah)-N(ah)

This week

Esta semana

ĒS-Tah SĒ-Mah-Nah

This month

Este mes

ĒS-TĒ MĒS

This year

Este año

ĒS-TĒ ahN-YO

Now

Ahora

ah-O-Rah

Soon

Pronto

PRON-TO

Later

Más tarde

MahS TahR-DĒ

Never

Nunca

NooN-Kah

WHO IS IT?

I

Yo

YⓄ

You (Formal)

Usted

(oo)S-T(ĕ)́D

Use this form of you with people you don't know well.

(Informal)

Tú

T(oo)

Use this form of you with people you know well.

We

Nosotros

NⓄ-SⓄ́-TŖⓄS

Use this form males only or males and females.

Nosotras

NⓄ-SⓄ́-TŖ(ah)S

Use this form for females only.

They

Ellos

(ĕ)́-YⓄS

A group of men only or a group of men and woman.

Ellas

(ĕ)́-Y(ah)S

A group of women only.

THE, A (AN), AND SOME

To use the correct form of **The**, **A (An)**, or **Some,** you must know if the Spanish word is masculine or feminine. Often you will have to guess! If you make a mistake, you will still be understood.

The

La

L(ah)

The before a singular feminine noun:
(La) girl is pretty.

Las

L(ah)S

The before a plural feminine noun:
(Las) girls are pretty.

El

(e)L

The before a singular masculine noun:
(El) man is handsome.

Los

L(o)S

The before a plural masculine noun:
(Los) men are handsome.

A or An

Un

(oo)N

A or **an** before a singular masculine noun:
He is (un) man.

Una

(oo)'-N(ah)

A or **an** before a singular feminine noun:
She is (una) woman.

Some

Unos

(oo)'-N(o)S

Some before plural masculine nouns:
(Unos) men

Unas

(oo)'-N(ah)S

Some before plural feminine nouns:
(Unas) women

USEFUL OPPOSITES

Near	**Far**
Cerca	Lejos
SⒺⓇ-Kⓐ	Lⓔ́-Hⓞ S
Here	**There**
Aquí	Ahí
ⓐ-KⒺⒺ́	ⓐ-ⒺⒺ́
Left	**Right**
Izquierda	Derecha
ⒺⒺ S-KⒺⒺ-ⓔ́Ⓡ-Dⓐ	Dⓔ́-Ⓡⓔ́-CHⓐ
A little	**A lot**
Un poquito	Mucho
ⓞⓞN Pⓞ-KⒺⒺ́-Tⓞ	Mⓞⓞ́-CHⓞ
More	**Less**
Más	Menos
Mⓐ S	Mⓔ́-Nⓞ S
Big	**Small**
Grande	Pequeño
GⓇⓐ́N-Dⓔ	Pⓔ́-Kⓔ́N-Yⓞ

Open

Abierto

@ah@-B@EE@-@ĕ@R-T@O@

Closed

Cerrado

S@ĕ@-B@ah@-D@O@

Cheap

Barato

B@ah@-B@ah@-T@O@

Expensive

Caro

K@ah@-B@O@

Clean

Limpio

L@EE@M-P@EE@-@O@

Dirty

Sucio

S@oo@-S@EE@-@O@

Good

Bueno

BW@ĕ@-N@O@

Bad

Malo

M@ah@-L@O@

Vacant

Desocupado

D@ĕ@-S@O@-K@oo@-P@ah@-D@O@

Occupied

Ocupado

@O@-K@oo@-P@ah@-D@O@

Right

Correcto

K@O@-B@ĕ@K-T@O@

Wrong

Incorrecto

@EE@N-K@O@-B@ĕ@K-T@O@

WORDS OF ENDEARMENT

I love you.

Te amo.

T⓮ ⓐⓗ-M⓪

My love

Mi amor

M⓮ⓔ ⓐⓗ-M⓪́B

My life

Mi vida

M⓮ⓔ V⓮ⓔ́-Dⓐⓗ

My friend (to a male)

Mi amigo

M⓮ⓔ ⓐⓗ-M⓮ⓔ́-G⓪

My friend (to a female)

Mi amiga

M⓮ⓔ ⓐⓗ-M⓮ⓔ́-Gⓐⓗ

Kiss me!

¡Bésame!

B⓮́-Sⓐⓗ-M⓮

WORDS OF ANGER

What do you want?

¿Qué quiere usted?

KĕĕKEE-ĕ-Rĕ ooS-TĕD

Leave me alone!

¡Déjeme en paz!

Dĕ-Hĕ-Mĕ ĕN Pah S

Go away!

¡Váyase!

VĪ-Yah-Sĕ

Stop bothering me!

¡No me moleste más!

No Mĕ Mo-Lĕ S-Tĕ Mah S

Be quiet!

¡Silencio!

SEE-Lĕ N-SEE-o

That's enough!

¡Basta!

Bah S-Tah

COMMON EXPRESSIONS

When you are at a loss for words but have the feeling you should say something, try one of these!

Who knows?

¿Quién sabe?

KEE-ёN Sah-Bё

That's the truth!

¡Es verdad!

ёS VёR-Dah'D

Sure!

¡Claro!

KLah-RO

Wow!

¡Caramba!

Kah-Rah'M-Bah

What's happening?

¿Qué pasa?

Kё Pah-Sah

I think so.

Creo que sí.

KRё-O Kё SEE

Cheers!

¡Salud!

S@h-L⊙⊙D

Good luck!

¡Buena suerte!

BW@̃-N@h SW@̃B-T@̃

With pleasure!

¡Con mucho gusto!

K⊙N M⊙⊙-CH⊙ G⊙⊙S-T⊙

My goodness!

¡Dios mío!

D@̃-⊙S M@̃-⊙

What a shame! / That's too bad!

¡Qué lástima!

K@̃ L@h̃S-T@̃-M@h

Well done! Bravo!

¡Olé!

⊙-L@̃

Never mind!

¡Olvídelo!

⊙L-V@̃-D@̃-L⊙

USEFUL COMMANDS

Stop!
¡Párese!
Pah-Rĕ-Sĕ
___

Go!
¡Vaya!
Vah-Yah
___

Wait!
¡Espérese!
ĕS-Pĕ-Rĕ-Sĕ
___

Hurry!
¡Apúrese!
ah-Poo-Rĕ-Sĕ
___

Slow down!
¡Despacio!
Dĕ-SPah-SEE-O
___

Come here!

¡Venga acá! (formal)   ¡Ven acá! (informal)
VĕN-Gah   ah-Kah   VĕN   ah-Kah
___

Help!
¡Socorro!
SO-KO-RO
___

EMERGENCIES

Fire!

¡Incendio!

ⒺN-SⒺN-DⒺ-Ⓞ

Emergency!

¡Emergencia!

Ⓔ-MⒺR-HⒺN-SⒺ-ah

Call the police!

¡Llame a la policía!

Yah-Mⓔ ah Lah PⓄ-Lⓔ-Sⓔ-ah

Call a doctor!

¡Llame un médico!

Yah-Mⓔ ⓄⓄN Mⓔ-Dⓔ-KⓄ

Call an ambulance!

¡Llame una ambulancia!

Yah-Mⓔ ⓄⓄ-Nah ahM-BⓄⓄ-LahN-SⓔE-ah

I need help!

¡Necesito ayuda!

Nⓔ-Sⓔ-Sⓔ-TⓄ ah-YⓄⓄ-Dah

ARRIVAL

Passing through customs should be easy since there are usually agents available who speak English. You may be asked how long you intend to stay and if you have anything to declare.

- Have your passport ready.

- Be sure all documents are up-to-date.

- While in a foreign country, it is wise to keep receipts for everything you buy.

- Be aware that many countries will charge a departure tax when you leave. Your travel agent should be able to find out if this affects you.

- If you have connecting flights, be sure to reconfirm them in advance.

- Make sure your luggage is clearly marked inside and out.

- Take valuables and medicines in carry-on bags.

SIGNS TO LOOK FOR:

ADUANA (Customs)

FRONTERA (Border)

CONTROL DE EQUIPAJE (Baggage control)

KEY WORDS

Baggage

El equipaje

ⓔL ⓔ-KⒺ-Pⓐ-Hⓔ

Customs

La aduana

Lⓐ ⓐ-DWⓐ-Nⓐ

Documents

Los documentos

LⓞS Dⓞ-Kⓞⓞ-Mⓔ́N-TⓞS

Passport

El pasaporte

ⓔL Pⓐ-Sⓐ-PⓞR-Tⓔ

Porter

El maletero   (Spain) El mozo

ⓔL Mⓐ-Lⓔ-Tⓔ́-Rⓞ   ⓔL Mⓞ́-THⓞ

Notice that in Spain the letter **z** is prounounced as **th**.

Tax

Los impuestos

LⓞS ⒺⒺM-PWⓔ́S-TⓞS

USEFUL PHRASES

Here is my passport.

Aquí tiene mi pasaporte.

ah-KEE TEE-ẽ-Nẽ MEE Pah-Sah-POʼR-Tẽ

I have nothing to declare.

No tengo nada que declarar.

NO TẽN-GO Nah-Dah
Kẽ Dẽ-KLah-RahʼR

I'm here on business.

Vengo de negocios.

Vẽn-GO Dẽ Nẽ-GOʼ-SEE-OS

I'm here on vacation.

Vengo de vacaciones.

Vẽn-GO Dẽ Vah-Kah-SEE-Oʼ-NẽS

Is there a problem?

¿Hay algún problema?

I ahL-GOOʼN PRO-BLẽʼ-Mah

PHRASEMAKER

I'll be staying...

Me voy a quedar...

Mē Voy ah Kē-DaR...

▶ **one week**

una semana

 oo-Nah Sē-Mah-Nah

▶ **two weeks**

dos semanas

DOS Sē-Mah-NahS

▶ **one month**

un mes

ooN MēS

▶ **two months**

dos meses

DOS MēS-ēS

USEFUL PHRASES

I need a porter!

¡Necesito un maletero!

Nẽ-Sẽ-SĒ-TO ⓄⓄN
Mⓐⓗ-Lẽ-Tẽ-ⓇO

These are my bags.

Estas son mis maletas.

ẼS-TⓐⓗS SⓄN MĒS Mⓐⓗ-Lẽ-TⓐⓗS

I'm missing a bag.

Me falta una maleta.

Mẽ FⓐⓗL-Tⓐⓗ ⓄⓄ-Nⓐⓗ Mⓐⓗ-Lẽ-Tⓐⓗ

Take my bags to the taxi, please.

Lleve mis maletas al taxi, por favor.

Yẽ-Vẽ MĒS Mⓐⓗ-Lẽ-TⓐⓗS ⓐⓗL
TⓐⓗK-SĒ PⓄR Fⓐⓗ-VOⓇ

Thank you. This is for you.

Gracias. Esto es para usted.

GⓇⓐⓗ-SĒ-ⓐⓗS
ẼS-TO ẼS Pⓐⓗ-Ⓡⓐⓗ ⓄⓄS-TẽD

PHRASEMAKER

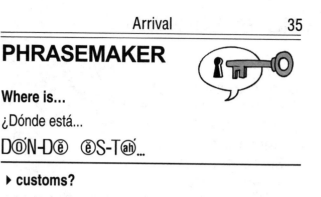

Where is...

¿Dónde está...

DŌN-Dē ēS-Tah...

▶ **customs?**

la aduana?

Lah ah-DWah-Nah

▶ **baggage claim?**

reclamación de equipaje?

Rē-KLah-Mah-SEE-ŌN
Dē ē-KEE-Pah-Hē

▶ **the money exchange?**

la casa de cambio?

Lah Kah-Sah Dē Kah M-BEE-O

▶ **the taxi stand?**

la parada de taxis?

Lah Pah-Rah-Dah Dē Tah K-SEES

▶ **the bus stop?**

la parada de autobuses?

Lah Pah-Rah-Dah Dē ow-TO-Boo-Sēs

HOTEL SURVIVAL

A wide selection of accommodations, ranging from the most basic to the most extravagant, are available wherever you travel in Spanish-speaking countries. When booking your room, find out what amenities are included for the price you pay.

- Make reservations well in advance and get written confirmation of your reservations before you leave home.

- Always have identification ready when checking in.

- Do not leave valuables, prescriptions, or cash in your room when you are not there!

- Electrical items like blow-dryers may need an adapter. Your hotel may be able to provide one, but to be safe, take one with you.

- Although a service charge is usually included on your bill, it is customary to tip maids, bellhops, and doormen.

KEY WORDS

Hotel
El hotel
ĚL O-TĚL

Bellman
El botones
ĚL BO-TŐ-NĚS

Maid
La camarera
Lah Kah-Mah-Rĕ-Rah

Message
El recado
ĚL Rĕ-Kah-DO

Reservation
La reservación
Lah Rĕ-SĚR-Vah-SEE-ÓN

Room service
El servicio de habitación
ĚL SĚR-VEE-SEE-O Dĕ
ah-BEE-Tah-SEE-ÓN

CHECKING IN

My name is...

Me llamo...

M℮ Yah-M⊙...

I have a reservation.

Tengo una reservación.

T℮́N-G⊙ ⊙⊙́-Nah R℮-S℮́R-Vah-S℮℮-⊙́N

If you don't have a reservation, just say **no** before this phrase.

Have you any vacancies?

¿Tiene alguna habitación libre?

T℮℮-℮́-N℮ ahL-G⊙⊙́-Nah

ah-B℮℮-Tah-S℮℮-⊙́N L℮℮-BR℮

What is the charge per night?

¿Cuánto es por noche?

KWah́N-T⊙ ℮S P⊙R N⊙́-CH℮

Is there room service?

¿Hay servicio de habitación?

⊙ S℮́R-V℮℮́-S℮℮-⊙ D℮

ah-B℮℮-Tah-S℮℮-⊙́N

PHRASEMAKER

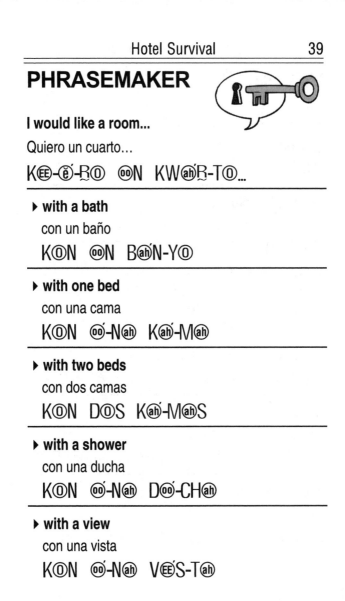

I would like a room...

Quiero un cuarto…

KEE-É-RO ooN KWah´R-TO…

▶ **with a bath**

con un baño

KON ooN Bah´N-YO

▶ **with one bed**

con una cama

KON oo´-Nah Kah´-Mah

▶ **with two beds**

con dos camas

KON DOS Kah´-MahS

▶ **with a shower**

con una ducha

KON oo´-Nah Doo´-CHah

▶ **with a view**

con una vista

KON oo´-Nah VEE´S-Tah

USEFUL PHRASES

Where is the dining room?

¿Dónde está el comedor?

DŌN-DĔ ĔS-Tah ĔL KŌ-MĔ-DŌR

Are meals included?

¿Están las comidas incluidas?

ĔS-Tah'N Lah'S KŌ-MĒ'-Dah'S
ĒN-KLoo-Ē'-Dah'S

What time is breakfast?

¿A qué hora es el desayuno?

ah KĔ Ō'-Rah ĔS ĔL
DĔ-Sah-Yoo'-NŌ

What time is lunch?

¿A qué hora es la comida?

ah KĔ Ō'-Rah ĔS Lah KŌ-MĒ'-Dah

What time is dinner?

¿A qué hora es la cena?

ah KĔ Ō'-Rah ĔS Lah SĔ'-Nah

My room key, please.

La llave de mi cuarto, por favor.

L@h Y@h-V@ D@ M@ KW@B-TO PFV

Are there any messages for me?

¿Tengo algún recado?

T@N-GO @hL-GooN B@-K@h-DO

Please wake me at…

Me despierta a las…

M@ D@S-P@-@B-T@h @h L@hS…

6:00
seis
S@S

6:30
seis y media
S@S @ M@-D@-@h

7:00
siete
S@-@-T@

7:30
siete y media
S@-@-T@ @ M@-D@-@h

8:00
ocho
O-CHO

8:30
ocho y media
O-CHO @ M@-D@-@h

9:00
nueve
NW@-V@

9:30
nueve y media
NW@-V@ @ M@-D@-@h

PHRASEMAKER

I need...

Necesito...

Nĕ-Sĕ-SĒ´-TO...

▸ **a babysitter**

una niñera

ōō´-Nah   NĒN-Yĕ´-Rah

▸ **a bellman**

un botones

ōōN   BO-TO´-Nĕs

▸ **more blankets**

más cobijas (mantas)

Mahs   KO-BĒ´-Hahs   (MahN-Tahs)

▸ **a hotel safe**

una caja fuerte

ōō´-Nah   Kah´-Hah   FWĕR-Tĕ

▸ **ice cubes**

cubitos de hielo

Kōō-BĒ´-TOS   Dĕ   Yĕ´-LO

▶ **an extra key**

otra llave

Ó-TRah Yah-Vě

▶ **a maid**

una camarera

ōō-Nah Kah-Mah-Rě-Bah

▶ **the manager**

el gerente

ěL Hě-Rěn-Tě

▶ **clean sheets**

sábanas limpias

Sah-Bah-NahS Lěm-Pee-ahS

▶ **soap**

jabón

Hah-Bón

▶ **toilet paper**

papel higiénico

Pah-Pěl ee-Hee-ě-Nee-Ko

▶ **more towels**

más toallas

MahS To-ah-YahS

PHRASEMAKER
(PROBLEMS)

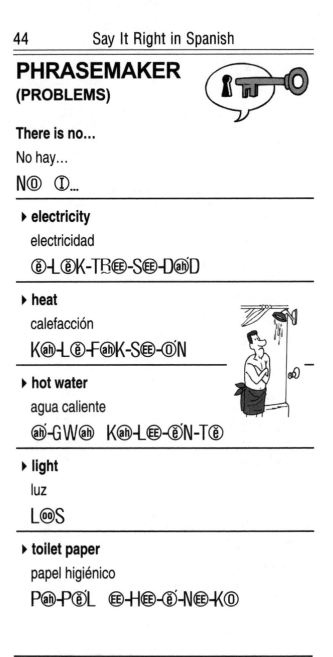

There is no...

No hay...

NO Ī...

▶ **electricity**

electricidad

Ē-LĒK-TRĒĒ-SĒĒ-Dah'D

▶ **heat**

calefacción

Kah-LĒ-Fah K-SĒĒ-O'N

▶ **hot water**

agua caliente

ah'-GWah　Kah-LĒĒ-ĒN-TĒ

▶ **light**

luz

Lōō S

▶ **toilet paper**

papel higiénico

Pah-PĒ'L　ĒĒ-HĒĒ-Ē'-NĒĒ-KO

PHRASEMAKER
(SPECIAL NEEDS)

Do you have...

¿Tiene...

TEE-ĕ-Nĕ...

▶ **an elevator?**

un ascensor?

ⓄⓄN ⓐⓐ-SⓔⓔN-SⓄⓇB

▶ **a ramp?**

una rampa?

ⓄⓄ-Nⓐⓐ BⓐⓐM-Pⓐⓐ

▶ **a wheel chair?**

una silla de ruedas?

ⓄⓄ-Nⓐⓐ SEE-Yⓐⓐ Dⓔ BⓄⓄ-ⓔ-DⓐⓐS

▶ **facilities for the disabled?**

facilidades para los inválidos?

Fⓐⓐ-SEE-LEE-Dⓐⓐ-DⓔS Pⓐⓐ-Bⓐⓐ LⓄS
EEN-Vⓐⓐ-LEE-DⓄS

CHECKING OUT

The bill, please.

La cuenta, por favor.

L@h KW@N-T@h PFV

Is this bill correct?

¿Está bien la cuenta?

@S-T@h B@-@N L@h KW@N-T@h

Do you accept credit cards?

¿Se aceptan tarjetas de crédito?

S@ @h-S@P-T@N T@R-H@-T@S D@
KR@-D@-T@

Could you have my luggage brought down?

¿Pueden bajarme el equipaje?

PW@-D@N B@h-H@R-M@ @L
@-K@-P@h-H@

Can you call a taxi for me?

¿Puede llamarme un taxi?

PWĕ-Dĕ YahMahR-Mĕ ooN
TahK-Sĕ

I had a very good time!

¡Me lo pasé muy bien!

Mĕ LO Pah-Sĕ MWĕ Bĕ-ĕN

Thanks for everything.

Gracias por todo.

GRah-Sĕ-ahS POR TO-DO

We'll see you next time.

Nos veremos la próxima.

NOS Vĕ-Rĕ-MOS Lah
PROK-Sĕ-Mah

Good-bye

Adiós

ah-Dĕ-OS

RESTAURANT SURVIVAL

The food available in Latin America and Spain is diverse. You will find a variety of tasty regional specialties. Mealtimes may be quite different than what you are used to!

- In Latin America and Spain, breakfast is usually served till 11 AM, lunch between 1 and 4 PM, and dinner from 9 PM till midnight. These are general guidelines and vary from country to country.

- In Spain, the Tasca bar offers appetizers or (**tapas**), a delicious way to fill the gap of time between lunch and dinner and a great way to meet people.

- A tip or service charge is often automatically included in your bill. Look for the words **Servicio Incluido**.

- In Mexico, avoid drinking tap water. Bottled water is available and recommended. In major hotels and restaurants, purified water is used; however, it is advisable to ask if your drink and or ice has been prepared with tap water.

KEY WORDS

Breakfast

El desayuno

ⓔL DⓔS-ⓐh-Yⓞⓞ´-Nⓞ

Lunch

El almuerzo

ⓔL ⓐhL-MWⓔ´R-Sⓞ

Dinner

La cena

Lⓐh Sⓔ´-Nⓐh

Waiter

El camarero

ⓔL Kⓐh-Mⓐh-Rⓔ´-Rⓞ

Waitress

La camarera

Lⓐh Kⓐh-Mⓐh-Rⓔ´-Rⓐh

Restaurant

El restaurante

ⓔL Rⓔ´S-Tⓞⓦ-RⓐhN-Tⓔ

USEFUL PHRASES

A table for...

Una mesa para...

ⓄⓄ-Nⓐ Mⓔ́-Sⓐ Pⓐ́-Ⓡⓐ...

2	4	6
dos	cuatro	seis
DⓄS	KWⓐ́-TⓇⓄ	S④S

The menu, please.

La carta, por favor.

Lⓐ Kⓐ́Ⓡ-Tⓐ PFV

Separate checks, please.

Cuentas separadas, por favor.

KWⓔ́N-Tⓐ S Sⓔ-Pⓐ-Ⓡⓐ́-Dⓐ S PFV

We are in a hurry.

Tenemos prisa.

Tⓔ-Nⓔ́-MⓄS PⓇⒺⒺ-Sⓐ

What do you recommend?

¿Qué recomienda la casa?

Kⓔ Ⓡⓔ-KⓄ-MⒺⒺ-ⓔ́N-Dⓐ Lⓐ Kⓐ́-Sⓐ

Please bring me...

Tráigame por favor...

TRÍ-G@ħ-M@... PFV

Please bring us...

Tráiganos por favor...

TRÍ-G@ħ-N@S... PFV

I'm hungry.

Tengo hambre.

T@N-G@   @ħM-BR@

I'm thirsty.

Tengo sed.

T@N-G@   S@D

Is service included?

¿Está incluido el servicio?

@S-T@ħ   @N-KL@-@-D@   @L
S@R-V@-S@-@

The bill, please.

La cuenta, por favor.

L@   KW@N-T@ħ   PFV

In Spain, the menu prices are required by law to include the service charge. It is customary to leave an additional tip if you are happy with the service!

PHRASEMAKER

Ordering beverages is easy and a great way to practice your Spanish! In many foreign countries you will have to request ice with your drinks.

Please bring me...

Tráigame, por favor...

TRⒾ-Gⓐⓗ-MⒺ... PFV

▶ **coffee**

un café

ⓄⓄN Kⓐⓗ-FⒺ

▶ **tea**

un té

ⓄⓄN TⒺ

▶ **with cream**

con crema

KⓄN KRⒺ-Mⓐⓗ

▶ **with sugar**

con azúcar

KⓄN ⓐⓗ-SⓄⓄ-KⓐⓗR

▶ **with lemon**

con limón

KⓄN LⒺⒺ-MⓄN

▶ **with ice**

con hielo

KⓄN YⒺ-LⓄ

Soft drinks

Los refrescos

LOS Bĕ-FRĔS-KOS

Milk

La leche

Lah LĔ-CHĔ

Hot chocolate

El chocolate

ĔL CHO-KO-Lah-TĔ

Juice

El jugo

ĔL HOO-GO

Orange juice

El jugo de naranja

ĔL HOO-GO DĔ Nah-Bah-N-Hah

Ice water

El agua fría

ĔL ah-GWah FREE-ah

Mineral water

El agua mineral

ĔL ah-GWah MEE-NĔ-Bah-L

AT THE BAR

Bartender

El cantinero

ⓔL KⓐN-TⒺⒺ-Nⓔ́-Ⓡ⊙

The wine list, please.

La lista de vinos, por favor.

Lⓐ LⒺⒺ́S-Tⓐ Dⓔ VⒺⒺ́-N⊙S PF

Cocktail

El cóctel

ⓔL K⊙́K-Tⓔ́L

On the rocks

Con hielo

K⊙N Yⓔ́-L⊙

Straight

Sin hielo

SⒺⒺN Yⓔ́-L⊙

With lemon

Con limón

K⊙N LⒺⒺ-M⊙́N

PHRASEMAKER

I would like a glass of...

Quisiera un vaso de...

KEE-SEE-é-Rah oON Vah-SO Dé...

▶ **champagne**

champaña

CHahM-Pah'N-Yah

▶ **beer**

cerveza

SéR-Vé-Sah

▶ **wine**

vino

VEE'-NO or BEE'-NO

You will often hear the Spanish letter **v** pronounced like a soft English **b**.

▶ **red wine**

vino tinto

VEE'-NO TEE'N-TO

▶ **white wine**

vino blanco

VEE'-NO BLah'N-KO

ORDERING BREAKFAST

In Latin America, breakfast can be extravagant. In Spain, breakfast is generally a simple meal consisting of coffee or tea and bread.

Bread

El pan

ⓔL Pⓐⓝ

Toast

El pan tostado

ⓔL Pⓐⓝ TⓄ-STⓐ́-DⓄ

with butter

con mantequilla

KⓄN Mⓐⓝ-Tⓔ-Kⓔ́E-Yⓐ

with jam

con mermelada

KⓄN Mⓔ́R-Mⓔ-Lⓐ́-Dⓐ

Cereal

El cereal

ⓔL Sⓔ-Rⓔ-ⓐ́L

PHRASEMAKER

I would like...

Quisiera...

KEE-SEE-ĕ́-Rah...

▶ **two eggs...**

dos huevos...

DOS WĕH-VOS...

▶ **scrambled**

revueltos

RĕH-VWĕ́L-TOS

▶ **fried**

fritos

FREE-TOS

▶ **with bacon**

con tocino

KON TO-SEE-NO

▶ **with ham**

con jamón

KON Hah-MON

▶ **with potatoes**

con papas

KON Pah́-PahS

con patatas (Spain)

KON Pah-Tah-TahS

LUNCH AND DINNER

Although you are encouraged to sample regional cuisines, it is important to be able to order foods you are familiar with. This section will provide words and phrases to help you.

I would like...

Quisiera...

KEE-SEE-ě-Rah...

We would like...

Quisiéramos...

KEE-SEE-ě-Rah-MOS

Bring us...

Nos trae...

NOS TRŎ-ě... PFV

The lady would like...

La señora quisiera...

Lah SěN-YO-Rah KEE-SEE-ě-Rah...

The gentleman would like...

El señor quisiera...

ěL SěN-YOB KEE-SEE-ě-Rah...

STARTERS

Appetizers
Los entremeses

LOS ĕN-TRĕ-Mĕ-SĕS

Bread and butter
El pan y la mantequilla

ĕL PahN EE Lah MahN-Tĕ-KEE-Yah

Cheese
El queso

ĕL Kĕ-SO

Fruit
La fruta

Lah FRoo-Tah

Salad
La ensalada

Lah ĕN-Sah-Lah-Dah

Soup
La sopa

Lah SO-Pah

MEATS

Bacon

El tocino

ⓔL TⓄ-SⒺⒺ´-NⓄ

Beef

La carne de res

Lⓐ Kⓐ´R-Nⓔ Dⓔ Rⓔ S

Beef steak

El bistec

ⓔL BⒺⒺ-STⓔ´K

Ham

El jamón

ⓔL Hⓐ-MⓄ´N

Lamb

El cordero

ⓔL KⓄR-Dⓔ´-RⓄ

Pork

La carne de puerco   Las carnitas (Mexico)

Lⓐ Kⓐ´R-Nⓔ Dⓔ PWⓔR-KⓄ

Lⓐ S Kⓐ´R-NⒺⒺ-Tⓐ S

Veal

La carne de ternera

Lⓐ Kⓐ´R-Nⓔ Dⓔ Tⓔ R-Nⓔ´-Rⓐ

POULTRY

Baked chicken

El pollo al horno

ēL PŌ-YŌ ahL ŌR-NŌ

Broiled chicken

El pollo a la parrilla

ēL PŌ-YŌ ah Lah Pah-BEE-Yah

Fried chicken

El pollo frito

ēL PŌ-YŌ FREE-TŌ

Duck

El pato

ēL Pah-TŌ

Goose

El ganso

ēL Gahn-SŌ

Turkey

El pavo   El guajolote (Mexico)

ēL Pah-VŌ   ēL GWah-HŌ-LŌ-Tē

SEAFOOD

Fish
El pescado
ⓔL PⓔS-Kⓐ-DⓄ

Lobster
La langosta
Lⓐ LⓐN-GⓄ-STⓐ

Oysters
Las ostras
LⓐS ⓄS-TRⓐS

Salmon
El salmón
ⓔL Sⓐ L-MⓄN

Shrimp
Los camarones
LⓄS Kⓐ-Mⓐ-RⓄ-NⓔS

Trout
La trucha
Lⓐ TRⓄ-CHⓐ

Tuna
El atún
ⓔL ⓐ-TⓄN

OTHER ENTREES

Sandwich
La torta (Latin America)   El bocadillo (Spain)

Lah TOR-Tah

ĕL BO-Kah-DEE-YO

Hot dog
El hot dog

ĕL Hah T DahG

Hamburger
La hamburguesa

Lah ah M-BOO R-Gĕ-Sah

French fries
Las papas fritas or Las patatas fritas

LahS Pah-PahS FREE-TahS

LahS Pah-Tah-TahS FREE-TahS

Pasta
La pasta

Lah PahS-Tah

Pizza
La pizza

Lah PEE T-Sah

VEGETABLES

Carrots

Las zanahorias

LahS Sah-Nah-O-REE-ahS

Corn

El maíz

eL Mah-EES

Mushrooms

Los hongos   Los champiñones (Spain)

LOS ON-GOS   LOS CHahM-PEEN-YO-NeS

Onions

Las cebollas

LahS SeB-BO-YahS

Potato

La papa   La patata (Spain)

Lah Pah-Pah   Lah Pah-Tah-Tah

Rice

El arroz

eL ah-BOS

Tomato

El tomate

eL TO-Mah-Te

FRUITS

Apple
La manzana
Lah Mahn-Sah-Nah

Banana
La banana
Lah Bah-Nah-Nah

Grapes
Las uvas
Lahs oo-Vahs

Lemon
El limón
el Lee-Mon

Orange
La naranja
Lah Nah-Rahn-Hah

Strawberry
La fresa
Lah FRe-Sah

Watermelon
La sandía
Lah Sahn-Dee-ah

DESSERT

Desserts

Los Postres

LOS POS-TRes

Apple pie

El pastel de manzana

eL Pah-STeL De Mahn-Sah-Nah

Cherry pie

El pastel de cereza

eL Pah-STeL De   Se-Re-Sah

Pastries

Los pasteles

LOS Pah-STe-Les

Candy

Los dulces

LOS Dool-Ses

Ice cream

La nieve   El helado (Spain)

Lah NEE-ĕ-Vĕ   ĕL ĕ-Lah-DO

Ice-cream cone

El barquillo de helado

ĕL Bah-KEE-YO Dĕ ĕ-Lah-DO

Chocolate

El chocolate

ĕL CHO-KO-Lah-Tĕ

Strawberry

La fresa

Lah FRĕ-Sah

Vanilla

La vainilla

Lah VI-NEE-Yah

CONDIMENTS

Butter
La mantequilla

L@h M@hN-T&-K&-Y@h

Ketchup
El ketchup

&L K&-CH@P

Mayonnaise
La mayonesa

L@h M@h-YO-N&-S@h

Mustard
La mostaza

L@h MOS-T@h-S@h

Salt
La sal

L@h S@hL

Pepper
La pimienta

L@h P&-M&-&N-T@h

Sugar
El azúcar

&L @h-Soo-K@hR

Vinegar and oil
El vinagre y aceite

&L V&-N@h-GR& & @h-S@-T&

SETTINGS

A cup
Una taza
-N T-S

A glass
Un vaso
N V-S

A spoon
Una cuchara
-N K-CH-R

A fork
Un tenedor
N T-N-DR

A knife
Un cuchillo
N K-CH-Y

A plate
Un plato
N PL-T

A napkin
Una servilleta
-N SR-V-Y-T

HOW DO YOU WANT IT COOKED?

Baked

Al horno

@L O'R-NO

Broiled

A la parrilla

@ L@ P@-REE'-Y@

Steamed

Al vapor

@L V@-PO'R

Fried

Frito

FREE'-TO

Rare

Poco cocida

PO'-KO KO-SEE'-D@

Medium

Término medio

TE'R-MEE-NO ME'-DEE-O

Well done

Bien cocida

BEE-E'N KO-SEE'-D@

PROBLEMS

I didn't order this.

No pedí esto.

NO Pĕ-DĒ ĕS-TO

Is the bill correct?

¿Está bien la cuenta?

ĕS-Tah BĒ-ĕN Lah KWĕN-Tah

Please bring me...

Tráigame, por favor...

TRĪ-Gah-Mĕ... PFV

GETTING AROUND

Getting around in a foreign country can be an adventure in itself! Taxi and bus drivers do not always speak English, so it is essential to be able to give simple directions. The words and phrases in this chapter will help you get where you're going.

- Negotiate the fare with your taxi driver in advance so there are no misunderstandings. Tell him where you want to go and find out exactly what he intends to charge.

- Never get in unmarked taxi cabs no matter where you are!

- Check with your travel agent about special rail passes which allow unlimited travel within a set period of time.

- If you are traveling by train in Europe, remember trains leave on time. Arrive early to allow time for ticket purchasing and checking in.

- There are several types of train transportation from **Talgos** (fast) to **Rápidos** (regular) and **Estrellas** (nighttime). **Regionales** travel regionally, **Cercanas** are local commuter trains, and **Largo** are long-distance trains.

KEY WORDS

Airport

El aeropuerto

ⓔL ⓐh-ⓔ-ℝⓄ-PWⓔℝ-TⓄ

Bus Station / Stop

La estación de autobuses
La parada de autobuses

Lⓐh ⓔ-STⓐh-Sⓔⓔ-ⓄN Dⓔ ⓞⓦ-TⓄ-Bⓞⓞ-SⓔS

Lⓐh Pⓐh-ℝⓐh-Dⓐh Dⓔ ⓞⓦ-TⓄ-Bⓞⓞ-SⓔS

Car Rental Agency

Una agencia de carros de alquiler

ⓞⓞN-ⓐh ⓐh-Hⓔ'N-Sⓔⓔ-ⓐh Dⓔ

Kⓐh-ℝⓄS Dⓔ ⓐh-Kⓔⓔ-Lⓔ'ℝ

Subway Station

La estación de metro

Lⓐh ⓔ-STⓐh-Sⓔⓔ-ⓄN Dⓔ Mⓔ'-TℝⓄ

Taxi Stand

La parada de taxis

Lⓐh Pⓐh-ℝⓐh-Dⓐh Dⓔ Tⓐh'K-Sⓔⓔ

Train Station

La estación de ferrocarriles

Lⓐh ⓔ-STⓐh-Sⓔⓔ-ⓄN Dⓔ

Fⓔ-ℝⓄ-Kⓐh-ℝⓔⓔL-ⓔS

AIR TRAVEL

Arrivals	**Departures**
Las llegadas	Las salidas
L@S Y€-G@-D@S	L@S S@-L€-D@S

Flight number

El número de vuelo

€L N©-M€-R© D€ VW@-L©

Airline

La línea aérea

L@ L€-N€-@ @-€-R€-@

The gate

La puerta

L@ PW€R-T@

Information

Información

€N-F©R-M@-S€-©N

Ticket (airline)

El boleto

€L B©-L€-T©

Reservations

Las reservaciones

L@S R€-S€R-V@-S€-©-N€S

PHRASEMAKER

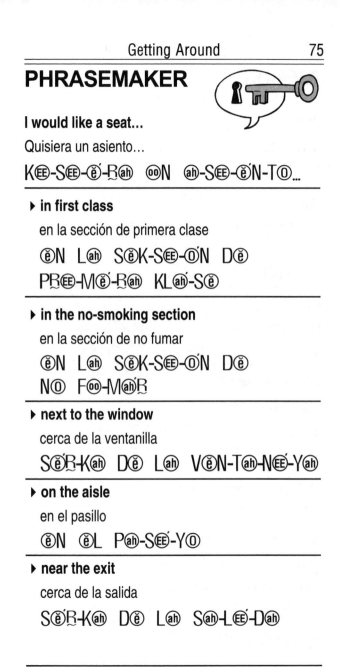

I would like a seat...

Quisiera un asiento...

KEE-SEE-ĕ-Rah ooN ah-SEE-ĕN-TO...

▸ **in first class**

en la sección de primera clase

ĕN Lah SĕK-SEE-ON Dĕ
PREE-Mĕ-Rah KLah-Sĕ

▸ **in the no-smoking section**

en la sección de no fumar

ĕN Lah SĕK-SEE-ON Dĕ
NO Foo-Mah'B

▸ **next to the window**

cerca de la ventanilla

SĕB-Kah Dĕ Lah VĕN-Tah-NEE-Yah

▸ **on the aisle**

en el pasillo

ĕN ĕL Pah-SEE-YO

▸ **near the exit**

cerca de la salida

SĕB-Kah Dĕ Lah Sah-LEE-Dah

BY BUS

Bus

El autobús   El camión (Mexico)

ⓔL ⓞⓦ-Tⓞ-Bⓞⓞ′S   ⓔL Kⓐ-MⒺⒺ-Ó′N

Where is the bus stop?

¿Dónde está la parada de autobuses?

DÓ′N-Dⓔ ⓔ′S-Tⓐ′ Lⓐ

Pⓐ-Rⓐ′-Dⓐ Dⓔ ⓞⓦ-Tⓞ-Bⓞⓞ′-SⓔS

Do you go to...?

¿Va usted a…?

Vⓐ ⓞⓞ-STⓔ′D ⓐ

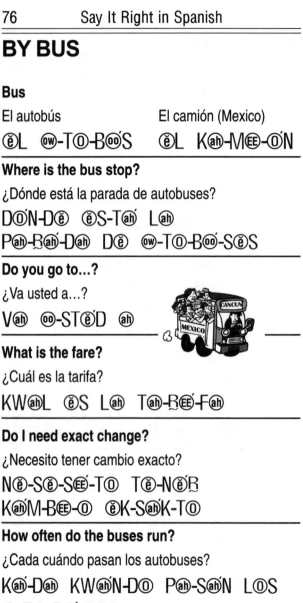

What is the fare?

¿Cuál es la tarifa?

KWⓐL ⓔ′S Lⓐ Tⓐ-RⒺⒺ′-Fⓐ

Do I need exact change?

¿Necesito tener cambio exacto?

Nⓔ-Sⓔ-SⒺⒺ′-Tⓞ Tⓔ-Nⓔ′R

Kⓐ′M-BⒺⒺ-Ⓞ ⓔK-Sⓐ′K-Tⓞ

How often do the buses run?

¿Cada cuándo pasan los autobuses?

Kⓐ′-Dⓐ KWⓐ′N-Dⓞ Pⓐ-Sⓐ′N LⓞS

ⓞⓦ-Tⓞ-Bⓞⓞ′-SⓔS

PHRASEMAKER

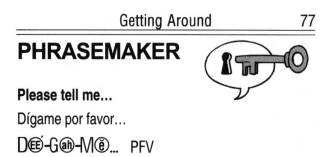

Please tell me...

Dígame por favor…

DĒĒ-Gah-Mē… PFV

▶ **which bus goes to...**

cuál autobús va para…

KWah-L ow-TO-Boo'S Vah Pah-Rah…

▶ **at what time does the bus leave**

a qué hora sale el autobús

ah Kē Ō-Rah Sah-Lē ēL
ow-TO-Boo'S

▶ **where the bus stop is**

dónde está la parada de autobuses

DŌN-Dē ēS-Tah Lah Pah-Rah-Dah
Dē ow-TO-Boo'-Sēs

▶ **when we are at...**

cuando estemos en…

KWah'N-DO ēS-Tē-MOS ēN…

▶ **where to get off**

dónde debo bajarme

DŌN-Dē Dē-BO Bah-Hah'R-Mē

BY CAR

Fill it up.

Llénelo.

YÉ-NÉ-LO

Can you help me?

¿Puede usted ayudarme?

PWÉ-DÉ ooS-TÉD ah-Yoo-DahR-MÉ

My car won't start.

Mi carro no arranca.

MEE Kah-RO NO ah-BahN-Kah

Can you fix it?

¿Pueden arreglarlo?

PWÉ-DÉN ah-RÉ-GLahR-LO

What will it cost?

¿Cuánto costará?

KWahN-TO KO-STah-Rah

How long will it take?

¿Cuánto tiempo durará?

KWahN-TO TEE-ÉM-PO Doo-Rah-Rah

PHRASEMAKER

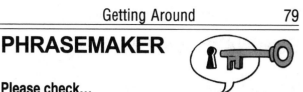

Please check...

Revise...

Rē-VĒ-Sē... PFV

▶ **the battery**

la batería

Lah Bah-Tē-RĒ-ah

▶ **the brakes**

los frenos

LOS FRē-NOS

▶ **the oil**

el aceite

ēL ah-SĀ-Tē

▶ **the tires**

las llantas

LahS Yah'N-TahS

▶ **the water**

el agua

ēL ah'-GWah

SUBWAYS AND TRAINS

Where is the subway station?

¿Dónde está el metro?

DON-De　eS-Tah　eL　Me-TRO

Where is the train station?

¿Dónde está la estación de ferrocarril?

DON-De　eS-Tah　Lah　eS-Tah-SEE-
ON　De　Fe-RO-Kah-BeL

A one-way ticket, please.

Un billete de ida, por favor.

OON　BEE-Ye-Te　De　EE-Dah　PFV

A round trip ticket

Un billete de ida y vuelta

OON　BEE-Ye-Te　De　EE-Dah　EE
VWeL-Tah　PFV

First class

Primera clase

PREE-Me-Bah　KLah-Se

Second class

Segunda clase

Se-GOON-Dah　KLah-Se

Which train do I take to go to...

¿Cuál tren tomo para ir a...?

KW@L TR@N TO-M@ P@-R@
@R @...

What is the fare?

¿Cuánto es la tarifa?

KW@N-T@ @S L@ T@-R@-F@

Is this seat taken?

¿Está ocupado este asiento?

@S-T@ @-K@-P@-D@
@S-T@ @-S@-@N-T@

Do I have to change trains?

¿Tengo que cambiar de tren?

T@N-G@ K@ K@M-B@-@R
D@ TR@N

Does this train stop at...

¿Se para este tren en...?

S@ P@-R@ @S-T@ TR@N @N...

Where are we?

¿Dónde estamos?

D@N-D@ @S-T@-M@S

BY TAXI

Can you call a taxi for me?

¿Me puede llamar un taxi?

M@ PW@-D@ Y@h-M@hR

@@N T@hK-S@@

Are you available?

¿Está usted libre?

@S-T@h @@S-T@D L@@-BR@

I want to go...

Quiero ir...

K@@-@-R@ @@R...

Stop here, please.

Pare aquí, por favor.

P@h-R@ @h-K@@ PFV

Please wait.

Espérese, por favor.

@-SP@-R@-S@ PFV

How much do I owe?

¿Cuánto le debo?

KW@hN-T@ L@ D@-B@

PHRASEMAKER

I would like to go...

Quisiera ir...

KEE-SEE-ĕ-Rah ĕR...

▶ **to this address**

a esta dirección

ah ĕS-Tah DEE-RĕK-SEE-ON

▶ **to the airport**

al aeropuerto

ahL ah-ĕ-RO-PWĕR-TO

▶ **to the bank**

al banco

ahL BahN-KO

▶ **to the hotel**

al hotel

ahL O-TĕL

▶ **to the hospital**

al hospital

ahL OS-PEE-TahL

▶ **to the subway station**

al metro

ahL Mĕ-TRO

SHOPPING

Whether you plan a major shopping spree or just need to purchase some basic necessities, the following information is useful.

- In Latin America and Spain, shops generally close in the afternoon for siesta. They re-open in the late afternoon and stay open into the night.

- You are likely to encounter an item called VAT (in Mexico IVA). This stands for Value-Added Tax. It is a tax which is quoted in the price of merchandise and services. Unlike other countries, Mexico's IVA is not refundable.

- In Spain, always inquire about VAT refund procedures at the time of purchase.

- Always keep receipts for everything you buy! This will be helpful in filling out Customs declaration when you return home.

SIGNS TO LOOK FOR:

ALMACEN (Department Store)

BAZAR (Department Store, Spain)

PANADERIA (Bakery)

MERCADO (Market)

SUPERMERCADO (Supermarket)

KEY WORDS

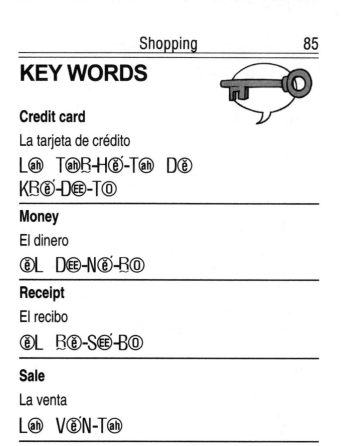

Credit card

La tarjeta de crédito

Lah Tah-R-Hě-Tah Dě
KRě-Děe-TO

Money

El dinero

ěL Děe-Ně-RO

Receipt

El recibo

ěL Rě-Sěe-BO

Sale

La venta

Lah Věn-Tah

Store

La tienda

Lah Těe-ěN-Dah

Traveler's check

El cheque de viajero

ěL CHě-Kě Dě Věe-ah-Hě-RO

USEFUL PHRASES

Do you sell...?

¿Vende usted...?

VĒN-DĒ ⊚⊚S-TĒD...

Do you have...?

¿Tiene usted...?

TĒ-Ē-NĒ ⊚⊚S-TĒD...

I want to buy...

Quisiera comprar...

KĒ-SĒ-Ē-Rah KOM-PRahR...

How much?

¿Cuánto es?

KWahN-TO ĒS

When are the shops open?

¿Cuándo se abren las tiendas?

KWahN-DO SĒ ah-BRĒN

Lah S TĒ-ĒN-DahS

No thank you.

No, gracias.

NO GRah-SĒ-ahS

I´m just looking.

Sólo estoy mirando.

SO-LO ES-Toy MEE-Bahn-DO

It's very expensive!

¡Es muy caro!

ES MWEE Kah-BO

Can't you give me a discount?

¿No me da una rebaja?

NO ME Dah oo-Nah BE-Bah-Hah

I'll take it!

¡Me lo llevo!

ME LO YE-VO

I'd like a receipt, please.

Quiero un recibo, por favor.

KEE-E-BO ooN BE-SEE-BO PFV

I want to return this.

Quiero devolver esto.

KEE-E-BO DE-VOL-VEB ES-TO

It doesn't fit.

No me viene.

NO ME VEE-E-NE

PHRASEMAKER

I'm looking for...

Busco...

B⍥S-K⍥...

▸ **a bakery**

una panadería

⍥-N⍐ P⍐-N⍐-D⍥-R⍥-⍐

▸ **a bank**

un banco

⍥N B⍐N-K⍥

▸ **a barber shop**

una peluquería

⍥-N⍐ P⍥-L⍥-K⍥-R⍥-⍐

▸ **a beauty shop**

un salón de belleza

⍥N S⍐-L⍥N D⍥ B⍥-Y⍥-S⍐

▸ **a camera shop**

una tienda de fotografía

⍥N-⍐ T⍥-⍥N-D⍐ D⍥
F⍥-T⍥-GR⍐-F⍥-⍐

▸ **a pharmacy**

una farmacia

⍥-N⍐ F⍐B-M⍐-S⍥-⍐

PHRASEMAKER

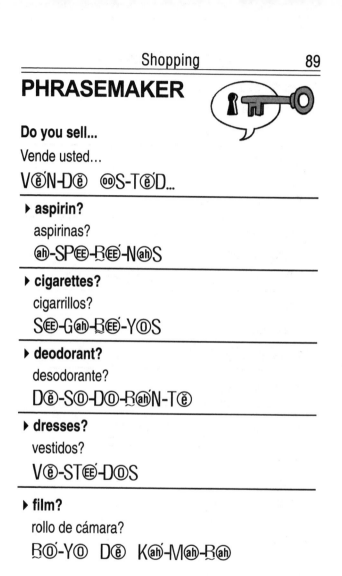

Do you sell...

Vende usted…

V**ẽ**N-D**ẽ** ⊚⊚S-T**ẽ**D...

▶ **aspirin?**

aspirinas?

ah-SP**EE**-R**EE**-N**ah**S

▶ **cigarettes?**

cigarrillos?

S**EE**-G**ah**-R**EE**-Y**⊙**S

▶ **deodorant?**

desodorante?

D**ẽ**-S**⊙**-D**⊙**-R**ah**N-T**ẽ**

▶ **dresses?**

vestidos?

V**ẽ**-ST**EE**-D**⊙**S

▶ **film?**

rollo de cámara?

R**⊙**-Y**⊙**   D**ẽ**   K**ah**-M**ah**-R**ah**

▶ **pantyhose?**

pantimedias?

P@N-T€€-M€́-D€€-@S

▶ **perfume?**

perfume?

P€R-F@-M€

▶ **razor blades?**

hojas de afeitar?

Ó-H@S D€ @-F€-T@R

▶ **shampoo?**

champú?

CH@M-P@

▶ **shaving cream?**

crema de afeitar?

KR€́-M@ D€ @-F€-T@R

▶ **shirts?**

camisas?

K@-M€́€-S@S

▶ **soap?**

jabón?

H@-BÓN

▶ **sunglasses?**

anteojos para el sol?

@N-T@-O'-H@S P@-R@ @L S@L

▶ **sunscreen?**

aceite para broncear?

@-S@'-T@ P@-R@
BR@N-S@-@'R

▶ **toothbrushes?**

cepillos de dientes?

S@-P@'-Y@S D@ D@-@'N-T@S

▶ **toothpaste?**

pasta de dientes?

P@'S-T@ D@ D@-@'N-T@S

▶ **water?** (bottled)

agua de botella?

@'-GW@ D@ B@-T@'-Y@

▶ **water?** (mineral)

agua mineral?

@'-GW@ M@-N@-R@'L

ESSENTIAL SERVICES

THE BANK

As a traveler in a foreign country your primary contact with banks will be to exchange money.

- Change enough funds before leaving home to pay for tips, food, and transportation to your final destination.

- It is also best to bring US dollar traveler's checks as well as US dollars in cash. You can exchange money in banks or **Casas de Cambio.**

- Current exchange rates are posted in banks and published daily in city newspapers.

- ATM machines are readily available in Mexico and are always open. Try to use ATMs in daylight hours. Credit cards are accepted widely.

- ATM machines are readily available in Spain and a good place to exchange money. Credit cards are accepted and purchases usually provide a favorable rate of exchange.

KEY WORDS

Bank

El banco

ⓔL BⓐⓃ-KⓄ

Exchange office

La casa de cambio

Lⓐ Kⓐ́-Sⓐ Dⓔ Kⓐ́M-BⒺ-Ⓞ

Money

El dinero

ⓔL DⒺ-Nⓔ́-RⓄ

Money order

El giro postal

ⓔL HⒺ́-RⓄ PⓄS-Tⓐ́L

Traveler's check

El cheque de viajero

ⓔL CHⓔ́-Kⓔ Dⓔ VⒺ-ⓐ-Hⓔ́-RⓄ

Currencies

Peso/Mexico	Euro/Spain	Sol/Perú
Pⓔ́-SⓄ	ⓞⓞ́-RⓄ	SⓄL

Balboa/Panamá	Colón/El Salvador	Peso/Chile
Bⓐ́L-BⓄ́-ⓐ	KⓄ-LⓄ́N	Pⓔ́-SⓄ

USEFUL PHRASES

Where is the bank?

¿Dónde está el banco?

DON-De eS-Tah eL Bahn-Ko

What time does the bank open?

¿A qué hora se abre el banco?

ah Ke O-Rah Se ah-BRe
eL Bahn-Ko

Where is the exchange office?

¿Dónde está la casa de cambio?

DON-De eS-Tah Lah Kah-Sah De
Kahm-Bee-O

What time does the exchange office open?

¿A qué hora se abre la casa de cambio?

ah Ke O-Rah Se ah-BRe Lah
Kah-Sah De Kahm-Bee-O

Can I change dollars here?

¿Puedo cambiar dólares aquí?

PWe-DO Kahm-Bee-ahR
DO-Lah-ReS ah-KEE

Can you change this?

¿Me puede cambiar esto?

Mẽ PWẽ-Dẽ KahM-BEE-ahR ẽS-TO

What is the exchange rate?

¿A cuánto está el cambio?

ah KWahN-TO ẽS-Tah ẽL
KahM-BEE-O

I would like large bills.

Quisiera billetes grandes.

KEE-SEE-ẽ-Rah BEE-Yẽ-TẽS
GRahN-DẽS

I would like small bills.

Quisiera billetes pequeños.

KEE-SEE-ẽ-Rah BEE-Yẽ-TẽS
Pẽ-KẽN-YOS

I need change.

Necesito cambio.

Nẽ-Sẽ-SEE-TO KahM-BEE-O

Do you have an ATM?

¿Tienen cajero automático?

TEE-ẽ-NẽN Kah-HẽR-O
ow-TO-Mah-TEE-KO

POST OFFICE

If you are planning to send letters and postcards, be sure to send them early so that you don't arrive home before they do. **Correo** identifies the post office.

KEY WORDS

Airmail

Por avión

PⓄB ⓐh-VⓔⒺ-ⓄN

Letter

La carta

Lⓐh Kⓐh̃B-Tⓐh

Post office

El correo

ⓔL KⓄ-Bⓔ-Ⓞ

Postcard

La tarjeta postal

Lⓐh Tⓐh̃B-Hⓔ-Tⓐh PⓄS-Tⓐh̃L

Stamp

El sello

ⓔL Sⓔ̃-YⓄ

USEFUL PHRASES

Where is the post office?

¿Dónde está el correo?

DON-De eS-Tah eL KO-Be-O

What time does the post office open?

¿A qué hora se abren los correos?

ah Ke O-Rah Se ahB-ReN
LOS KO-Be-OS

I need stamps.

Necesito unos sellos.

Ne-Se-SEE-TO oo-NOS Se-YOS

I need an envelope.

Necesito un sobre.

Ne-Se-SEE-TO ooN SO-BRe

I need a pen.

Necesito una pluma.

Ne-Se-SEE-TO oo-Nah PLoo-Mah

TELEPHONE

Placing phone calls in a foreign
country can be a test of will and
stamina! Besides the obvious
language barriers, service can vary greatly from
one town to the next.

- If you have a choice, do not call from your
  hotel room. Service charges can add a hefty
  amount to your bill. If you use your hotel for
  long distance or international calls, use a
  Calling Card. This will cost you less than hotel
  charges; however, a fee may still be charged.

- In Spain try to get to the CENTRAL
  TELEFONICA (CTNE). Here you can get
  assistance placing your call. You pay as soon
  as the call is completed.

- Calls can be made at telephone call centers
  and paid afterwards. There are also telephones
  in bars which cost more to use.

- In Mexico, you can purchase calling cards in
  stores, supermarkets, and newsstands. They
  can be used in "yellow" Telmex/Ladatel phone
  booths.

KEY WORDS

Information

Información

EN-FOR-Mah-SEE-ON

Long distance

Larga distancia

LahR-Gah DEES-TahN-SEE-ah

Operator

La operadora

Lah O-Pe-Rah-DOR-ah

Phone book

La guía telefónica

Lah GEE-ah Te-Le-FO-NEE-Kah

Public telephone

Teléfono público

Te-Le-FO-NO POOB-LEE-KO

Telephone

El teléfono

eL Te-Le-FO-NO

USEFUL PHRASES

May I use your telephone?

¿Puedo usar su teléfono?

PWĕ-DO ⓞⓞ-Sah'R Sⓞⓞ
Tĕ-Lĕ'-FO-NO

Operator, I don't speak Spanish.

Operadora, no hablo español.

Ⓞ-Pĕ-Rah-DO'R-ah NO ah'B-LO
ĕS-Pah'N-YO'L

I would like to make a long-distance call.

Quisiera hacer una llamada de larga distancia.

KⒺⒺ-SⒺⒺ-ĕ'-Rah ah-Sĕ'R ⓞⓞ-Nah
Yah-Mah'-Dah Dĕ Lah'R-Gah
DⒺⒺS-Tah'NSⒺⒺ-ah

I would like to make a call to the United States.

Quisiera hacer una llamada a los Estados Unidos.

KⒺⒺ-SⒺⒺ-ĕ'-Rah ah-Sĕ'R ⓞⓞ-Nah
Yah-Mah'-Dah ah LOS ĕS-Tah'-DOS
ⓞⓞ-NⒺⒺ'-DOS

I want to call this number...

Quiero llamar a este número...

KEE-é-RO Yah-MahB ah é-S-Té
NOO-MÉ-RO...

SIGHTSEEING AND ENTERTAINMENT

In most cities and towns in Spanish-speaking countries, you will find tourist information offices. Here you can usually obtain brochures, maps, historical information, bus and train schedules.

CITIES IN MEXICO

Ciudad de México
SEE-oo-DahD DÐ MÐ-HEE-KO

Acapulco
ah-Kah-PooL-KO

Cancún
KahN-KooN

CITIES IN SOUTH AMERICA

Buenos Aires
BWÐ-NOS Ī-RÐS

Santiago
SahN-TEE-ah-GO

Bogotá
BO-GO-Tah

Lima
LEE-Mah

CITIES IN SPAIN

Madrid
Mah-DREED

Barcelona
BahB-THÐ-LO-Nah

Sevilla (Seville)
SÐ-VEE-Yah

Pamplona
PahM-PLO-Nah

KEY WORDS

Admission

La admisión

L@h @hD-M€€-S€€-O'N

Map

El mapa

€L M@h-P@h

Reservation

La reservación

L@h R€-S€R-V@h-S€€-O'N

Ticket

El boleto

€L BO-L€-TO

El billete

€L B€€-Y€-T€

Tour

La excursión

L@h €KS-KOOR-S€€-O'N

Tour guide

El guía turístico

€L G€€-@h TOO-R€€S-T€€-KO

USEFUL PHRASES

Where is the tourist office?

¿Dónde está la oficina de turismo?

DÓN-Dẽ ẽS-Tah̓ Lah̓

O-FEE-SEE-Nah Dẽ TOO-REEZ-MO

Is there a tour to...?

¿Hay una excursión a...?

I ōō-Nah ẽKS-KOOR-SEE-ÓN ah...

Where do I buy a ticket?

¿Dónde compro la entrada?

DÓN-Dẽ KÓM-PRO Lah

ẽN-TRah̓-Dah

How much does the tour cost?

¿Cuánto cuesta la excursión?

KWah̓N-TO KWẽS-Tah Lah

ẽKS-KOOR-SEE-ÓN

How long does the tour take?

¿Cuánto dura la excursión?

KWah̓N-TO DOō-Rah Lah

ẽKS-KOOR-SEE-ÓN

Does the guide speak English?

¿Habla inglés el guía?

ah-BLah EEN-GLĕS ĕL GEE-ah

Are children free?

¿Pagan los niños?

Pah-GahN LOS NEEN-YOS

What time does the show start?

¿A qué hora empieza la función?

ah Kĕ O-Rah ĕM-PEE-ĕ-Sah Lah
FooN-SEE-ON

Do I need reservations?

¿Necesito una reserva?

Nĕ-Sĕ-SEE-TO oo-Nah Rĕ-SĕR-Vah

Where can we go dancing?

¿Dónde está la disco?

DON-Dĕ ĕS-Tah Lah DEES-KO

Is there a minimum cover charge?

¿Hay un cargo mínimo?

I ooN Kah-B-GO MEE-NEE-MO

PHRASEMAKER

May I invite you...

¿Quisiera invitarla…

KEE-SEE-ĕ́-Rah EEN-VEE-Tah́R-Lah…

▶ **to a concert?**

a un concierto?

ah ooN KON-SEE-ĕ́R-TO

▶ **to dance?**

a bailar?

ah BI-Lah́R

▶ **to dinner?**

a cenar?

ah Sĕ́-Nah́R

▶ **to the movies?**

al cine?

ahL SEE-Nĕ́

▶ **to the theater?**

al teatro?

ahL Tĕ́-ah́-TRO

PHRASEMAKER

Where can I find...

¿Dónde se encuentra...

DⓄN-Dⓔ Sⓔ ⓔN-KWⓔN-TRⓐ...

▶ **a health club?**

un gimnasio?

ⓞⓞN HⓔⓔM-Nⓐ-Sⓔⓔ-Ⓞ

▶ **a swimming pool?**

una piscina?

ⓞⓞ-Nⓐ Pⓔⓔ-Sⓔⓔ-Nⓐ

▶ **a tennis court?**

una cancha de tenis?

ⓞⓞ-Nⓐ Kⓐ'N-CHⓐ Dⓔ Tⓔ-NⓔⓔS

▶ **a golf course?**

un campo de golf?

ⓞⓞN Kⓐ'M-PⓄ Dⓔ GⓄLF

HEALTH

Hopefully you will not need medical attention on your trip. If you do, it is important to communicate basic information regarding your condition.

- Check with your insurance company before leaving home to find out if you are covered in a foreign country. You may want to purchase traveler's insurance before leaving home.

- If you take prescription medicine, carry your prescription with you. Have your prescriptions translated before you leave home.

- Take a small first-aid kit with you.

- Your embassy or consulate should be able to assist you in finding health care.

- In Mexico, some pharmacies are open 24 hours and others close around 10:00 PM.

- Some hotels can recommend English-speaking doctors and others have a doctor on call.

- In Spain, a **GREEN CROSS** indicates pharmacy, where you can get basic medical information. A list of local pharmacies, open at night, is posted in the shop.

KEY WORDS

Ambulance

La ambulancia

Lah ahM-Boo-Lahñ-SEE-ah

Dentist

El dentista

EL DeN-TEE'S-Tah

Doctor

El médico

EL ME-DEE-KO

Emergency

La emergencia

Lah E-MER-HEN-SEE-ah

Hospital

El hospital

EL OS-PEE-Tah'L

Prescription

La receta

Lah RE-SE-Tah

USEFUL PHRASES

I am sick.

Estoy enfermo. (male) Estoy enferma. (female)

ⓔS-Tⓞý ⓔN-Fⓔ́R-Mⓞ (ⓐh)

I need a doctor.

Necesito ayuda.

Nⓔ́-Sⓔ́-Sⓔⓔ́-Tⓞ ⓐh-Yⓞⓞ́-Dⓐh

It's an emergency!

¡Es una emergencia!

ⓔS ⓞⓞ́-Nⓐh ⓔ́-Mⓔ́R-Hⓔ́N-Sⓔⓔ-ⓐh

Where is the nearest hospital?

¿Dónde está el hospital más cercano?

Dⓞ́N-Dⓔ̈ ⓔS-Tⓐh́ ⓔL ⓞS-Pⓔⓔ-Tⓐh́L Mⓐ́hS Sⓔ̈R-Kⓐh́-Nⓞ

Call an ambulance!

¡Llame una ambulancia!

Yⓐh́-Mⓔ̈ ⓞⓞ́-Nⓐh ⓐhM-Bⓞⓞ-Lⓐh́N-Sⓔⓔ-ⓐh

I'm allergic to...

Tengo alergias a…

TÊN-GO ah-LÊR-HEE-ahS ah...

I'm pregnant.

Estoy embarazada.

ÊS-Toy ÊM-Bah-Rah-Sah-Dah

I'm diabetic.

Soy diabético. (male)   Soy diabética. (female)

Soy DEE-ah-BÊ-TEE-KO (ah)

I have a heart condition.

Sufro del corazón.

Soo-FRO DÊL KO-Rah-SON

I have high blood pressure.

Tengo la tensión alta.

TÊN-GO Lah TÊN-SEE-ON ahL-Tah

I have low blood pressure.

Tengo la tensión baja.

TÊN-GO Lah TÊN-SEE-ON Bah-Hah

PHRASEMAKER

I need...

Necesito...

Nꬲ-Sꬲ-Sᴇᴇ́-Tⓞ...

▶ **a doctor**

un médico

ⓞN Mꬲ́-Dᴇᴇ-Kⓞ

▶ **a dentist**

un dentista

ⓞN DꬲN-Tᴇᴇ́S-Tⓐⓗ

▶ **a nurse**

una enfermera

ⓞⓞ́-Nⓐⓗ ꬲN-Fꬲ́R-Mꬲ́-Rⓐⓗ

▶ **an optician**

un optometrista

ⓞN ⓞP-Tⓞ-Mꬲ-TRᴇᴇ́S-Tⓐⓗ

▶ **a pharmacist**

un farmacéutico

ⓞN FⓐⓗR-Mⓐⓗ-Sⓞⓞ́-Tᴇᴇ-Kⓞ

PHRASEMAKER
(AT THE PHARMACY)

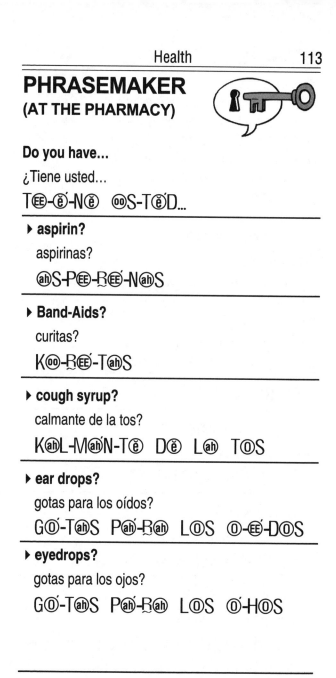

Do you have...

¿Tiene usted...

TEE-ê-Nê ooS-TêfD...

▶ **aspirin?**

aspirinas?

ahS-PEE-REE-NahS

▶ **Band-Aids?**

curitas?

Koo-REE-TahS

▶ **cough syrup?**

calmante de la tos?

KahL-MahN-Tê Dê Lah TOS

▶ **ear drops?**

gotas para los oídos?

GO-TahS Pah-Rah LOS O-EE-DOS

▶ **eyedrops?**

gotas para los ojos?

GO-TahS Pah-Rah LOS O-HOS

BUSINESS TRAVEL

It is important to show appreciation and interest in another person's language and culture, particularly when doing business. A few well-pronounced phrases can make a great impression.

I have an appointment.

Tengo una cita.

TĔN-GŌ ōō-Nah SĒĒ-Tah

Here is my card.

Aquí tiene mi tarjeta personal.

ah-KĒĒ TĒĒ-Ĕ-NĔ MĒĒ Tah-R-HĔ-Tah PĔR-SŌ-NahL

Can we get an interpreter?

¿Hay un intérprete?

Ī ōōN ĒN-TĔR-PRĔ-TĔ

May I speak to Mr...?

¿Se encuentra el señor...?

SĔ ĔN-KWĔN-TRah ĔL SĔN-YŌR...

May I speak to Mrs...?

¿Se encuentra la señora...?

SĔ ĔN-KWĔN-TRah Lah SĔN-YŌ-Rah...

KEY WORDS

Appointment
La cita
L@h S€€-T@h

Meeting
La reunión
L@h R€-oo-N-Y@N

Marketing
El mercado técnico
@L M€R-K@-D@ T€K-N€€-K@

Presentation
La presentación
L@h PR€-S@N-T@h-S€€-@N

Sales
Las ventas
L@hS V€N-T@hS

PHRASEMAKER

I need…

Necesito…

Nẽ-Sẽ-Sẽ´-TO…

▶ **a computer**

una computadora
un ordenador (Spain)

oo´-Nah KOM-Poo-Tah-DO´-Rah

ooN OB-Dẽ-Nah-DOR´

▶ **a copy machine**

una máquina para hacer copias

oo´-Nah Mah´-KEE-Nah Pah´-Rah

ah-SẽR KO´-PEE-ahS

▶ **a conference room**

un salón de conferencias

ooN Sah-LON´ Dẽ KON-Fẽ-Rẽ´N-SEE-ahS

▶ **a fax machine**

un fax

ooN Fah KS

▶ **an interpreter**

un intérprete

ooN EEN-TẽR-PRẽ´-Tẽ

▶ **a lawyer**

un abogado

ⓄⓄN ⓐʰ-BⓄ-Gⓐʰ-DⓄ

▶ **a notary**

un notario

ⓄⓄN NⓄ-Tⓐʰ-RⒺⒺ-Ⓞ

▶ **overnight delivery**

entrega expresa

entrega inmediata (Spain)

ⒺN-TRⒺ-Gⓐʰ ⒺKS-PRⒺ-Sⓐʰ

ⒺN-TRⒺ-Gⓐʰ ⒺⒺN-MⒺ-DⒺⒺ-ⓐʰ-Tⓐʰ

▶ **paper**

papel

Pⓐʰ-PⒺL

▶ **pen**

pluma

PLⓄⓄ-Mⓐʰ

▶ **pencil**

lápiz

Lⓐʰ-PⒺⒺZ

▶ **a secretary**

una secretaria

ⓄⓄ-Nⓐʰ SⒺ-KRⒺ-Tⓐʰ-RⒺⒺ-ⓐʰ

GENERAL INFORMATION

Climate in Latin America and Spain is diverse. Weather is largely affected by altitude and terrain.

SEASONS

Spring

La primavera

L@h PR@E-M@h-V@-R@h

Summer

El verano

@L V@-R@h-N@

Autumn

El otoño

@L @-T@N-Y@

Winter

El invierno

@L @N-V@E-@R-N@

THE DAYS

Monday
lunes
Lōō-NēS

Tuesday
martes
MahR-TēS

Wednesday
miércoles
Mee-ēR-Ko-LēS

Thursday
jueves
Hōō-ē-VēS

Friday
viernes
Vee-ēR-NēS

Saturday
sábado
Sah-Bah-Do

Sunday
domingo
Do-MeeN-Go

THE MONTHS

January
enero
Ⓔ-NⒺ-ⓇⓄ

February
febrero
Fⓔ-BⓇⓔ-ⓇⓄ

March
marzo
Ⓜⓐ́Ⓡ-SⓄ

April
abril
ⓐⓗ-BⓇⒺ́L

May
mayo
Ⓜⓐ́-YⓄ

June
junio
HⓄⓄ-NⒺⒺ-Ⓞ

July
julio
HⓄⓄ́-LⒺⒺ-Ⓞ

August
agosto
ⓐⓗ-GⓄ́S-TⓄ

September
septiembre
SⓔP-TⒺⒺ-ⓔ́M-BⓇⓔ

October
octubre
ⓄK-TⓄⓄ-BⓇⓔ

November
noviembre
NⓄ-VⒺⒺ-ⓔ́M-BⓇⓔ

December
diciembre
DⒺⒺ-SⒺⒺ-ⓔ́M-BⓇⓔ

COLORS

Black	**White**
Negro	Blanco
NĒ-GRO	BLäN-KO
Blue	**Brown**
Azul	Café
äh-SOOL	Käh-FĒ
Gray	**Gold**
Gris	Oro
GREES	O-RO
Orange	**Yellow**
Anaranjado	Amarillo
äh-Näh-RähN-Häh-DO	äh-Mäh-REE-YO
Red	**Green**
Rojo	Verde
RO-HO	VĒR-DĒ
Pink	**Purple**
Rosado	Morado
RO-Säh-DO	MO-Räh-DO

NUMBERS

0	**1**	**2**
Cero	Uno	Dos
SĔ-RO	oo-NO	DOS

3	**4**	**5**
Tres	Cuatro	Cinco
TRĔS	KWah-TRO	SĒN-KO

6	**7**	**8**
Seis	Siete	Ocho
SAS	SĒ-ĕ-Tĕ	O-CHO

9	**10**	**11**
Nueve	Diez	Once
NWĕ-Vĕ	DĒ-ĕS	ON-Sĕ

12	**13**	**14**
Doce	Trece	Catorce
DO-Sĕ	TRĔ-Sĕ	Kah-TOR-Sĕ

15	**16**	
Quince	Dieciséis	
KĒN-Sĕ	DĒ-ĕS-ĒE-SAS	

17

Diecisiete

DĒ-ĕS-ĒE-SĒ-ĕ-Tĕ

18

Dieciocho

DEE-ēS-EE-Ó-CHO

19	**20**
Diecinueve	Veinte
DEE-ēS-EE-NWē-Vē	VĀN-Tē

30	**40**
Treinta	Cuarenta
TRĀN-Tah	KWah-RḗN-Tah

50	**60**
Cincuenta	Sesenta
SEEN-KWḗN-Tah	Sē-SḗN-Tah

70	**80**
Setenta	Ochenta
Sē-TḗN-Tah	O-CHḗN-Tah

90	**100**
Noventa	Cien
NO-VḗN-Tah	SEE-ḗN

1000	**1,000,000**
Mil	Millón
MEEL	MEE-YÓN

DICTIONARY

Each English entry is followed by the Spanish word and the EPLS translation. Gender of nouns is indicated by (m) for masculine and (f) for feminine.

Plural is indicated by (/pl). Adjectives are shown in their masculine form, as common practice dictates. Adjectives and some nouns that end in **o** or **os** can usually be changed to feminine by changing the ending to **a** or **as**. Verbs appear in infinitive form, indicated by (to).

A

a, an un (m), una (f) ⓞⓞN ⓞⓞ-Nⓐ

a lot mucho Mⓞⓞ-CHⓞ

able (to be) poder Pⓞ-Dⓔ̈R

above sobre Sⓞ-BRⓔ̈

accident accidente (m) ⓐK-Sⓔⓔ-Dⓔ̈N-Tⓔ̈

accommodation alojamiento (m)
    ⓐ-Lⓞ-Hⓐ-Mⓔⓔ-ⓔ̈N-Tⓞ

account cuenta (f) KWⓔ̈N-Tⓐ

address dirección (f) Dⓔⓔ-Rⓔ̈K-Sⓔⓔ-ⓞN

admission admisión (f) ⓐD-Mⓔⓔ-Sⓔⓔ-ⓞN

afraid tener miedo Tⓔ̈N-ⓔ̈R Mⓔⓔ-ⓔ̈-Dⓞ

after después Dⓔ̈S-PWⓔ̈S

afternoon tarde (f) T@B-D@

air-conditioning aire acondicionado (m)

    Ⓘ-Rⓔ @-KON-Dⓔⓔ-Sⓔⓔ-O-N@-DO

aircraft avión (m) @-Vⓔⓔ-ON

airline línea aérea (f) Lⓔⓔ-Nⓔ-@ @-ⓔ-Rⓔ-@

airport aeropuerto (m) @-ⓔ-RO-PWⓔB-TO

aisle pasillo (m) P@-Sⓔⓔ-YO

all todo TO-DO

almost casi K@-Sⓔⓔ

alone solo SO-LO

also también T@M-Bⓔⓔ-ⓔN

always siempre Sⓔⓔ-ⓔM-PRⓔ

ambulance ambulancia (f) @M-Boo-L@N-Sⓔⓔ-@

American americano (m) @-Mⓔ-Rⓔⓔ-K@-NO

    americana (f) @-Mⓔ-Rⓔⓔ-K@-N@

and y ⓔⓔ

another otro O-TRO

anything algo @L-GO

apartment apartamento (m) @-P@B-T@-MⓔN-TO

appetizers entremeses (m/pl) ⓔN-TRⓔ-Mⓔ-SⓔS

apple manzana (f) M@N-S@-N@

appointment cita (f)　SEE-Tah

April abril (m)　ah-BREEL

arrival llegada (f)　YE-Gah-Dah

arrive (to) llegar　YE-GahR

ashtray cenicero (m)　SE-NEE-SE-RO

aspirin aspirina (f)　ah-SPEE-REE-Nah

attention ¡atención!　ah-TEN-SEE-ON

August agosto (m)　ah-GOS-TO

Australia Australia　ow-STRA-LEE-uh

Australian Australiano (m)　ow-STRA-LEE-uh-NO

　　Australiana (f)　ow-STRA-LEE-uh-Nah

author autor (m)　ow-TOR

automobile automóvil (m)　ow-TO-MO-VEEL

autumn otoño (m)　O-TON-YO

avenue avenida (f)　ah-VEN-EE-Dah

awful horrible　O-REE-BLE

B

baby bebé (m)　BE-BE

babysitter niñera (f)　NEEN-YE-Rah

bacon tocino (m)　TO-SEE-NO

bad malo MAH-LO

bag maleta (f) MAH-LE-Tah

baggage equipaje (m) E-KEE-PAH-HE

baked al horno ahL OR-NO

bakery panadería (f) PAH-NAH-DE-REE-ah

banana plátano (m) PLAH-TAH-NO

Band-Aid curita (f) KOO-REE-Tah

bank banco (m) BAHN-KO

barbershop peluquería (f) PE-LOO-KE-REE-ah

bartender cantinero (m) KAHN-TEE-NE-RO

bath baño (m) BAHN-YO

bathing suit traje de baño (m)

TRAH-HE DE BAHN-YO

bathroom baño (m) BAHN-YO

battery batería (f), pila (f) BAH-TE-REE-ah, PEE-Lah

beach playa (f) PLAH-Yah

beautiful bello BE-YO

beauty shop salón de belleza (m)

SAH-LON DE BE-YE-Sah

bed cama (f) KAH-Mah

beef carne de res (f) KAHR-NE DE RES

beer cerveza (f)   SⒺR-VⒺ́-Sⓐ

bellman botones (m)   BⓄ-TⓄ́-NⒺS

belt cinturón (m)   SⒺⒺN-TⓄⓄ-RⓄ́N

big grande   GRⓐN-DⒺ

bill cuenta (f)   KWⒺN-Tⓐ

black negro   NⒺ́-GRⓄ

blanket cobija (f)   KⓄ-BⒺⒺ́-Hⓐ

        manta (f) (Spain)   Mⓐ́N-Tⓐ

blue azul   ⓐ-SⓄⓄL

boat barco (m)   Bⓐ́R-KⓄ

book libro (m)   LⒺⒺ́-BRⓄ

bookstore librería (f)   LⒺⒺ-BRⒺ-RⒺⒺ́-ⓐ

border frontera (f)   FRⓄN-TⒺ́-Rⓐ

boy muchacho (m)   MⓄⓄ-CHⓐ́-CHⓄ

bracelet pulsera (f)   PⓄⓄL-SⒺ́-Rⓐ

brake freno (m)   FRⒺ́-NⓄ

bread pan (m)   Pⓐ́N

breakfast desayuno (m)   DⒺ-Sⓐ-YⓄⓄ́-NⓄ

broiled a la parrilla   ⓐ Lⓐ Pⓐ-RⒺⒺ́-Yⓐ

brown café   Kⓐ-FⒺ́

brush cepillo (m)   SⒺ-PⒺⒺ́-YⓄ

building edificio (m) ĕ-DEE-FEE-SEE-O

bus autobús (m) ow-TO-BooS

bus station estación de autobuses (f)

    ĕ-STah-SEE-ON Dĕ ow-TO-Boo-SĕS

bus stop parada de autobuses (f)

    Pah-Rah-Dah Dĕ ow-TO-Boo-SĕS

business negocios (m) Nĕ-GO-SEE-OS

butter mantequilla (f) MahN-Tĕ-KĔ-Yah

buy (to) comprar KOM-PRahR

C

cab taxi (m) TahK-SEE

call (to) llamar Yah-MahR

camera cámara (f) Kah-Mah-Rah

Canada Canadá Kah-Nah-Dah

Canadian el canadiense (m) ĕL Kah-Nah-DEE-ĕN-Sĕ

    (f) la canadiense Lah Kah-Nah-DEE-ĕN-Sĕ

candy dulce (m) DooL-Sĕ

car carro (m), coche (m) automóvil (m)

    Kah-RO, KO-CHĕ, ow-TO-MO-VĕL

carrot zanahoria (f) Sah-NO-REE-ah

castle castillo (m) Kah-STĔ-YO

cathedral catedral (f)   Kah-Te-DRahL

celebration celebración (f)   Se-Le-BRah-SEE-ON

center centro   SeN-TRO

cereal cereal (m)   Se-Re-ahL

chair silla (f)   SEE-Yah

champagne champaña (m)   CHahM-PahN-Yah

change (to) cambiar   KahM-BEE-ahR

change (money) cambio (m)   KahM-BEE-O

cheap barato   Bah-Bah-TO

check (restaurant bill) cheque (m)   CHe-Ke

cheers! ¡salud!   Sah-LooD

cheese queso (m)   Ke-SO

chicken pollo (m)   PO-YO

child niño (m), niña (f)   NeeN-YO,   NeeN-Yah

chocolate chocolate   CHO-KO-Lah-Te

church iglesia (f)   EE-GLe-SEE-ah

cigar puro (m)   Poo-BO

cigarette cigarrillo (m)   SEE-Gah-BEE-YO

city ciudad (f)   SEE-oo-DahD

clean limpio   LeeM-PEE-O

close (to) cerrar SÉ-RahR

closed cerrado SÉ-Rah-DO

clothes ropa (f) RO-Pah

cocktail cóctel (m) KOK-TÉL

coffee café (m) Kah-FÉ

cold (temperature) frío FREÉ-O

comb peine (m) PÁ-NÉ

come (to) venir VÉ-NÉR

company compañía (f) KOM-PahN-YÉÉ-ah

computer computadora (f) KOM-Poo-Tah-DÓ-Rah
    ordenador (m) (Spain) OR-DÉ-Nah-DOR

concert concierto (m) KON-SÉÉ-ÉR-TO

condom profiláctico (m) PRO-FÉÉ-LahC-TÉÉ-KO

conference conferencia (f) KON-FÉ-RÉN-SÉÉ-ah

conference room salón de conferencias (m)
    Sah-LÓN DÉ KON-FÉ-RÉN-SÉÉ-ahS

congratulations felicitaciones (f/pl)
    FÉ-LÉÉ-SÉÉ-Tah-SÉÉ-Ó-NÉS

copy machine máquina para hacer copias (f)
    Mah-KÉÉ-Nah Pah-Rah ah-SÉR KO-PÉÉ-ahS
    Xerox (m) ZÉÉ-RahKS

corn maíz (m)   M@h-@S

cough syrup calmante de la tos (m)

K@L-M@N-T@ D@ L@ T@S

cover charge cargo mínimo (m)

K@R-G@ M@-N@-M@

crab cangrejo (m)   K@N-GR@-H@

cream crema (f)   KR@-M@

credit card tarjeta de crédito (f)

T@R-H@-T@ D@ KR@-D@-T@

cup taza (f)   T@-S@

customs aduana (f)   @-DW@-N@

D

dance (to) bailar   B@-L@R

dangerous peligroso   P@-L@-GR@-S@

date (calender) fecha (f)   F@-CH@

day día (m)   D@-@

December diciembre (m)   D@-S@-@M-BR@

delicious delicioso   D@-L@-S@-@-S@

delighted encantado   @N-K@N-T@-D@

dentist dentista (m)   D@N-T@S-T@

deodorant desodorante (m)   D@-S@-D@-R@N-T@

department store almacén (m) ⓐL-Mⓐ-Sⓔ́N

departure salida (f) Sⓐ-Lⓔ́-Dⓐ

dessert postre (m) Pⓞ́S-TRⓔ

detour desviación (f) Dⓔ́S-Vⓔⓐ-Sⓔ-Óⓝ

diabetic diabético (m) Dⓔ-ⓐ-Bⓔ́-Tⓔ-Kⓞ

diarrhea diarrea (f) Dⓔ-ⓐ-Rⓔ́-ⓐ

dictionary diccionario (m) Dⓔ́K-Sⓔ-Ⓞ-Nⓐ-Rⓔ-Ⓞ

dinner cena (f) Sⓔ́-Nⓐ

dining room comedor (m) Kⓞ-Mⓔ-Dⓞ́R

direction dirección (f) Dⓔ-Rⓔ́K-Sⓔ-Óⓝ

dirty sucio Sⓞⓞ-Sⓔ-Ⓞ

disabled inválido (m) ⓔN-Vⓐ́-Lⓔ-Dⓞ

discount descuento (m) Dⓔ́S-KWⓔ́N-Tⓞ
  rebaja (f) Rⓔ-Bⓐ́-Hⓐ

distance distancia (f) Dⓔ́S-Tⓐ̀N-Sⓔ-ⓐ

doctor médico (m) Mⓔ́-Dⓔ-Kⓞ

document documento (m) Dⓞ-Kⓞⓞ-Mⓔ́N-Tⓞ

dollar dólar (m) Dⓞ́-Lⓐ̀R

down abajo ⓐ-Bⓐ́-Hⓞ

downtown el centro ⓔL Sⓔ́N-TRⓞ

dress vestido (m) Vⓔ́S-Tⓔ́-Dⓞ

drink (to) beber Bĕ-Bĕʀ

drive (to) manejar Mah-Nĕ-Hahʀ

drugstore farmacia (f) Fahʀ-Mah-Sĕĕ-ah

dry cleaner tintorería (f) TĕĕN-Tō-Rĕ-Rĕĕ-ah

duck pato (m) Pah-Tō

E

ear oreja (f), oído (m) Ō-Rĕ-Hah, Ō-ĕĕ-Dō

ear drops gotas para los oídos (f/pl)

   Gō-Tahs Pah-Rah Lōs Ō-ĕĕ-Dōs

early temprano Tĕm-PRah-Nō

east este (m) ĕS-Tĕ

easy fácil Fah-SĕĕL

eat (to) comer Kō-Mĕʀ

egg huevo (m) Wĕ-Vō

eggs (fried) huevos fritos (m/pl)

   Wĕ-Vōs FRĕĕ-Tōs

eggs (scrambled) huevos revueltos (m/pl)

   Wĕ-Vōs Rĕ-VWĕL-Tōs

electricity electricidad (f) ĕ-Lĕk-TRĕĕ-Sĕĕ-Dahd

elevator ascensor (m) ah-SĕN-Sōʀ

embassy embajada (f) ĕM-Bah-Hah-Dah

emergency emergencia (f) ĕ-MĔR-HĔN-SĒE-ah

England Inglaterra (f) ĔEN-GLah-TĔ-Rah

English inglés (m) ĔEN-GLĔS

enough! ¡Basta! Bah'S-Tah

entrance entrada (f) ĔN-TRah-Dah

envelope sobre (m) SO-BRĕ

evening tarde (f) Tah'R-Dĕ

everything todo TO-DO

excellent excelente ĕK-Sĕ-LĔN-Tĕ

excuse me perdón PĕR-DO'N

exit salida (f) Sah-LĔE-Dah

expensive caro Kah'-RO

eye ojo (m) O'-HO

eyedrops gotas para los ojos (f/pl)
    GO-Tah'S Pah-Rah LOS O'-HOS

F

face cara (f) Kah'-Rah

far lejos LĔ'-HOS

fare billete (m) BĔE-Yĕ'-Tĕ

fast rápido Bah'-PĔE-DO

fax, fax machine fax (m) Fah'KS

February febrero (m) FĕH-BRĕH-RO

few poco PO-KO

film (movie) película (f) Pĕ-Lĕ-KOO-Lah

film (camera) rollo de cámara (m)

      RO-YO Dĕ Kah-Mah-Rah

fine muy bien MWĔĔ BĔĔ-ĕN

finger dedo (m) Dĕ-DO

fire fuego (m) FWĕ-GO

fire! ¡incendio! ĔĔN-Sĕ̈N-Dĕ-O

fire extinguisher extintor (m) ĔKS-Tĕ̈N-TOR

first primero PRĔĔ-Mĕ-RO

fish pescado (m) Pĕ̈S-Kah-DO

flight vuelo (m) VWĕ-LO

florist shop florería (f) FLO-Rĕ-Rĕ́-ah

flower flor (f) FLOR

food comida (f) KO-Mĕĕ-Dah

foot pie (m) Pĕĕ-ĕ̈

fork tenedor (m) Tĕ̈-Nĕ̈-DOR

french fries papas fritas (f/pl) Pah-Pah S FRĔĔ-Tah S

      patatas fritas (Spain) Pah-Tah-Tah S FRĔĔ-Tah S

fresh fresco FRĕ̈S-KO

Friday viernes (m)   VEE-ÉR-NÉS

fried frito   FREE-TO

friend amigo (m), amiga (f)
ah-MEE-GO, ah-MEE-Gah

fruit fruta (f)   FROO-Tah

funny gracioso   GRah-SEE-Ó-SO

G

gas station gasolinera (f)   Gah-SO-LEE-NÉ-Rah

gasoline petróleo (m)   PÉ-TRÓ-LÉ-O

gate puerta (f)   PWÉR-Tah

gentleman caballero (m)   Kah-Bah-YÉ-RO

gift regalo (m)   RÉ-Gah-LO

girl muchacha (f)   MOO-CHah-CHah

glass (drinking) vaso (m)   Vah-SO

glasses (eye) lentes (m/pl)   LÉN-TÉS

glove guante (m)   GWahN-TÉ

go vaya   Vah-Yah

gold oro (m)   Ó-RO

golf golf (m)   GOLF

golf course campo de golf (m)
KahM-PO DÉ GOLF

good bueno BWⒺ-NⓄ

good-bye adiós ⓐⓗ-DⒺⒺ-Ⓞ′S

goose ganso (m) GⓐⓗN-SⓄ

grape uva (f) ⓄⓄ′-Vⓐⓗ

grateful agradecido ⓐⓗ-GRⓐⓗ-DⒺ-SⒺⒺ-DⓄ

gray gris GRⒺⒺS

green verde VⒺR-DⒺ

grocery store tienda de comestibles (f)

　　　TⒺⒺ-ⒺN-Dⓐⓗ DⒺ KⓄ-MⒺS-TⒺⒺ-BLⒺS

group grupo (m) GRⓄⓄ′-PⓄ

guide guía (m) GⒺⒺ′-ⓐⓗ

H

hair cabello (m) Kⓐⓗ-BⒺ′-YⓄ

hairbrush cepillo (m) SⒺ-PⒺⒺ′-YⓄ

haircut corte de pelo (m)

　　　KⓄR-TⒺ DⒺ Pⓐ′-LⓄ

ham jamón Hⓐⓗ-MⓄ′N

hamburger hamburguesa (f) ⓐⓗM-BⓄⓄR-GⒺ′-Sⓐⓗ

hand la mano (f) Lⓐⓗ Mⓐⓗ-NⓄ

happy feliz FⒺ-LⒺⒺ′S

have (to) tener TⒺN-ⒺR

he él ēL

head cabeza (f) Kah-Bē-Sah

headache dolor de cabeza (m)

DO-LOR Dē Cah-Bē-Sah

health club gimnasio (m) HEEM-Nah-SEE-O

club (m) KLooB

heart corazón (m) KO-Rah-SON

heart condition Sufro del corazón (m)

Sooo-FRO DēL KO-Rah-SON

heat calefacción (f) Kah-Lē-Fah-K-SEE-ON

hello hola O-Lah

help! ¡socorro! SO-KO-RO

here aquí ah-KEE

holiday día feriado (m) DēE-ah Fē-REE-ah-DO

hospital hospital (m) OS-PEE-Tah-L

hot dog hot dog (m) ēL Hah-T Dah-G

hotel hotel (m) O-TēL

hour hora (f) O-Rah

how ¿cómo? KO-MO / ¿cuándo? KWah-N-DO

hurry up! ¡apúrese! ah-Poo-Rē-Sē

husband esposo ēS-PO-SO

I

I yo   YO

ice hielo (m)   YĒ-LO

ice cream nieve (f)   NEE-Ē-VĒ

  helado (m) (Spain)   Ē-LAH-DO

ice cubes cubitos de hielo (m/pl)

  KOO-BĒ-TOS DĒ YĒ-LO

ill enfermo   ĒN-FĒR-MO

important importante   ĒM-POR-TAHN-TĒ

indigestion indigestión (f)

  ĒN-DEE-HĒS-TEE-YON

information información (f)

  ĒN-FOR-MAH-SEE-ON

inn posada (f)   PO-SAH-DAH

interpreter intérprete (m)   ĒN-TĒR-PRĒ-TĒ

J

jacket chaqueta (f)   CHAH-KĒ-TAH

jam mermelada (f)   MĒR-MĒ-LAH-DAH

January enero (m)   Ē-NĒ-RO

jewelry joyas (f)   HOY-AHS

jewelry store joyería (f) Hoy-é-REE-ah

job trabajo (m) TRah-Bah-HO

juice jugo (m) Hoo-GO

July julio (m) Hoo-LEE-O

June junio (m) Hoo-NEE-O

K

ketchup ketchup (m) Kéh-CHoop

key llave (f) Yah-Véh

kiss beso (m) Béh-SO

knife cuchillo (m) Koo-CHEE-YO

L

ladies' restroom servicios de señoras (m/pl)
SéR-VEE-SEE-OS Déh SéN-YO-Rahs

lady dama (f) Dah-Mah

lamb cordero (m) KOR-Déh-RO

language idioma (m) EE-DEE-O-Mah

large grande GRahN-Déh

late tarde TahR-Déh

laundry lavandería (f) Lah-VahN-Déh-REE-ah

lawyer abogado (m) ah-BO-Gah-DO

left (direction) izquierdo EES-KEE-ER-DO

leg pierna (f) PEE-ER-Nah

lemon limón agrio (m) LEE-MON ah-GREE-O

less menos ME-NOS

letter carta (f) Kah-B-Tah

lettuce lechuga (f) LE-CHOO-Gah

light luz (f) LOOS

like, I me gusta ME GOOS-Tah

lip labio (m) Lah-BEE-O

lipstick pintura de labios (f)

    PEEN-TOO-Rah DE Lah-BEE-OS

little (amount) poquito PO-KEE-TO

little (size) pequeño PE-KEN-YO

live (to) vivir VEE-VEER

lobster langosta (f) Lah-N-GOS-Tah

long largo Lah-B-GO

lost perdido PER-DEE-DO

love amor (m) ah-MOR

luck suerte (f) SWER-TE

luggage equipaje (m) E-KEE-Pah-HE

lunch almuerzo (m) ahL-MWER-SO

M

maid camarera (f) Kah-Mah-RĒ-Rah

mail correo (m) KO-RĒ-O

makeup maquillaje (m) Mah-KEE-Yah-HĒ

man hombre (m) ŌM-BRĒ

manager gerente (m) HĒ-RĒN-TĒ

map mapa (m) Mah-Pah

March marzo (m) Mahr-SO

market mercado (m) MĒR-Kah-DO

match (light) cerillo (m), fósforo (m)

SĒ-RĒE-YO, FŌS-FO-RO

May mayo (m) Mah-YO

mayonnaise mayonesa (f) Mah-YO-NĒ-Sah

meal comida (f) KO-MĒE-Dah

meat carne (f) Kahr-NĒ

mechanic mecánico (m) MĒ-Kah-NĒE-KO

medicine medicina (f) MĒ-DĒE-SĒE-Nah

meeting reunión (f) RĒ-oo-NĒE-ŌN

mens' restroom servicios de señores (m/pl)

SĒR-VĒE-SĒE-OS DĒ SĒN-YO-RĒS

menu menú (m) MĒ-Noo

message recado (m)   Rē-Kah́-DO

milk leche (f)   Lē-CHē

mineral water agua mineral (m)

    ah́-GWah   MEE-Nē-Bah́L

minute minuto (m)   MEE-Noo-́TO

Miss señorita (f)   SēN-YO-Bēe-Tah

mistake error (f)   ē-BŌB

misunderstanding equivocación (f)

    ē-KEE-VO-Kah-SEE-ŌN

moment momento (m)   MO-MēN-TO

Monday lunes (m)   Loó-NēS

money dinero (m)   DEE-Nē-BO

month mes (m)   MēS

monument monumento (m)   MO-Noo-MēN-TO

more más   Mah́S

morning mañana (f)   Mah́N-Yah́-Nah

mosque mezquita (f)   MēS-KEé-Tah

mother madre (f)   Mah́-DBē

mountain montaña (f)   MON-Tah́N-Yah

movies cine (m)   SEé-Nē

Mr. señor (m)   SēN-YŌB

Mrs. señora (f)   SēN-YŌ-Bah

much, too demasiado Dⓔ-Mⓐ-SⒺ-ⓐ-Dⓞ

museum museo (m) Mⓞⓞ-Sⓔ-ⓞ

mushrooms hongos (m/pl) ⓞN-GⓞS

music música (f) Mⓞⓞ-SⒺ-Kⓐ

mustard mostaza (f) MⓞS-Tⓐ-Sⓐ

N

nail polish esmalte para uñas (m)
ⓔS-MⓐL-Tⓔ Pⓐ-Rⓐ ⓞⓞN-YⓐS

name nombre (m) NⓞM-BRⓔ

napkin servilleta (f) SⓔR-VⒺ-Yⓔ-Tⓐ

napkins (sanitary) almohadillas higiénicas (f)
ⓐL-Mⓞ-Hⓐ-DⒺ-YⓐS Ⓔ-HⒺ-ⓔ-NⒺ-KⓐS

near cerca SⓔR-Kⓐ

neck cuello (m) KWⓔ-Yⓞ

need, I necesito Nⓔ-Sⓔ-SⒺ-Tⓞ

never nunca NⓞⓞN-Kⓐ

newspaper periódico (m) Pⓔ-RⒺ-ⓞ-DⒺ-Kⓞ

news stand quiosco de periódicos (m)
KⒺ-ⓞS-Kⓞ Dⓔ Pⓔ-RⒺ-ⓞ-DⒺ-KⓞS

night noche (f)   NO-CHe

nightclub cabaret (m)   Kah-Bah-ReT

no no   NO

no smoking no fumar   NO Foo-Mah'R

noon mediodía (m)   Me-Dee-O-Dee-ah

north norte (m)   NOR-Te

notary notario (m)   NO-Tah-Ree-O

November noviembre (m)   NO-Vee-eM-BRe

now ahora   ah-O-Rah

number número (m)   Noo-Me-RO

nurse enfermera (f)   eN-FeR-Me-Bah

O

occupied ocupado   O-Koo-Pah-DO

ocean océano   O-Se-ah-NO

October octubre (m)   OK-Too-BRe

officer oficial (m)   O-Fee-See-ahL

oil aceite (m)   ah-SA-Te

omelet tortilla de huevos (f)

   TOR-Te-Yah De We-VOS

one-way (traffic) una vía   oo-Nah Vee-ah

onion cebolla (f)   Se-BO-Yah

open (to) abrar ah-BRahR

opera ópera (f) O'-Pē-Rah

operator operadora (f) O-Pē-Rah-DO'R-ah

optician optometrista (m) OP-TO-Mē-TREE'S-Tah

orange (color) anaranjado ah-Nah-Rah'N-Hah'-DO

orange (fruit) naranja (f) Nah-Rah'N-Hah

order (to) ordenar OR-Dē-Nah'R

original original O-REE-HEE-Nah'L

owner dueño (m) DWē'N-YO

oyster ostra (f) O'S-TRah

P

package paquete (m) Pah-Kē-Tē

paid pagado Pah-Gah'-DO

pain dolor (m) DO-LO'R

painting pintura (f) PEEN-Too'-Rah

pantyhose pantimedias (f/pl)
    Pah'N-TEE-Mē-DEE-ahS

paper papel (m) Pah-Pē'L

partner (business) socio (m) SO'-SEE-O

party fiesta (f) FEE-ē'S-Tah

passenger pasajero (m) Pah-Sah-Hё-RO

passport pasaporte (m) Pah-Sah-POR-Tё

pasta pasta (f) Pah́S-Tah

pastry pastel (m) Pah-STёL

pen pluma (f) PLoo-Mah

pencil lápiz (m) Lah-PёёS

pepper pimienta (f) Pёё-Mёё-ё́N-Tah

perfume perfume (m) Pё̇B-Foo-Mё

person persona (f) Pё̇B-SO-Nah

person to person personal Pё̇B-SO-NahL

pharmacist farmacéutico (m)

    Fah-Mah-Soo-Tёё-KO

pharmacy farmacia (f) Fah-Mah-Sёё-ah

phone book guía telefónica (f)

    Gёё-ah Tё-Lё-FO-Nёё-Kah

photo foto (f) FO-TO

photographer fotógrafo (m) FO-TO-GRah-FO

pie pastel de (follow with name of filling)

    Pah-STёL Dё

pillow almohada (f) ahL-MO-ah-Dah

pink rosado RO-Sah-DO

pizza pizza (f) PᴇᴇT-Sah or Pᴇᴇ-Sah

plastic plástico (m) PLahS-Tᴇᴇ-KO

plate plato (m) PLah-TO

please por favor POR Fah-VOR

pleasure placer (m) PLah-SᴇR

police policía (f) PO-Lᴇᴇ-Sᴇᴇ-ah

police station comisaría (f) KO-Mᴇᴇ-Sah-Rᴇᴇ-ah

pork carne de puerco (f) KahR-Nᴇ Dᴇ PWᴇR-KO

porter maletero (m) Mah-Lᴇ-Tᴇ-RO

post office correo (m) KO-Rᴇ-O

postcard tarjeta postal (f) TahR-Hᴇ-Tah POS-TahL

potato papa (f), patata (f) (Spain)

   Pah-Pah, Pah-Tah-Tah

pregnant embarazada ᴇM-Bah-Rah-Sah-Dah

prescription receta (f) Rᴇ-Sᴇ-Tah

price precio (m) PRᴇ-Sᴇᴇ-O

problem problema (m) PRO-BLᴇ-Mah

profession profesión (f) PRO-Fᴇ-Sᴇᴇ-ON

public público POOB-Lᴇᴇ-KO

public telephone teléfono público (m)

   Tᴇ-Lᴇ-FO-NO POOB-Lᴇᴇ-KO

purified purificada Poo-Ree-Fee-Cah-Dah

purple morado MO-Rah-DO

purse bolsa (f) BOL-Sah

Q

quality calidad (f) Kah-Lee-DahD

question pregunta (f) PRe-Goon-Tah

quickly rápido Rah-Pee-DO

quiet callado Kah-Yah-DO

quiet, be! ¡silencio! See-Len-See-O

R

radio radio (f) Rah-Dee-O

railroad ferrocarril (m) Fe-RO-Kah-Reel

rain lluvia (f) Yoo-Vee-ah

raincoat impermeable (m)

　　　Eem-Per-Me-ah-BLe

ramp rampa (f) RahM-Pah

rare (cooked) poco cocida PO-KO KO-See-Dah

razor blades hojas de afeitar (f/pl)

　　　O-Hahs De ah-Fe-TahR

ready listo (m), lista (f) Lees-TO, Lees-Tah

receipt recibo (m) Rē-SĒ-BŌ

recommend (to) recomendar Rē-KŌ-MĒN-DₐₕR

red rojo RŌ-HŌ

repeat! ¡repita! Rē-PĒ-Tₐₕ

reservation reserva (f), reservación (f)

    Rē-SĒR-Vₐₕ / Rē-SĒR-Vₐₕ-SĒ-ŌN

restaurant restaurante (m) Rēs-Tow-RₐₕN-Tē

return devolver Dē-VŌL-VĒR

rice arroz (m) ₐₕ-RŌS

rich rico Rēē-KŌ

right (correct) correcto KŌ-Rēk-TŌ

right (direction) derecha Dē-Rē-CHₐₕ

road camino (m) Kₐₕ-MĒĒ-NŌ

room cuarto (m) KWₐₕR-TŌ

round trip ida y vuelta ĒĒ-Dₐₕ ĒĒ VWēL-Tₐₕ

S

safe (in a hotel) caja fuerte (f)

    Kₐₕ-Hₐₕ FWēR-Tē

salad ensalada (f) ēN-Sₐₕ-Lₐₕ-Dₐₕ

sale venta (f) VēN-Tₐₕ

salmon salmón (m) SaL-MON

salt sal (f) SaL

sandwich torta (f) TOR-Tah

    bocadillo (m) (Spain) BO-Kah-DEE-YO

Saturday sábado (m) Sah-Bah-DO

scissors tijeras (f/pl) TEE-HO-RahS

sculpture escultura (f) ES-KooL-Too-Rah

seafood mariscos (m/pl) Mah-BEES-KOS

season estación (f) ES-Tah-SEE-ON

seat asiento (m) ah-SEE-EN-TO

secretary secretaria (f) SE-KRE-Tah-REE-ah

section sección (f) SEK-SEE-ON

September septiembre (m) SEP-TEE-EM-BRE

service servicio (m) SER-VEE-SEE-O

several varios Vah-REE-OS

shampoo champú (m) CHahM-Poo

sheets (bed) sábanas (f/pl) Sah-Bah-NahS

shirt camisa (f) Kah-MEE-Sah

shoe zapato (m) Sah-Pah-TO

shoe store zapatería (f) Sah-Pah-TE-REE-ah

shopping center centro comercial (m)

    SEN-TRO KO-MER-SEE-ahL

shower ducha (f) DOO-CHah

shrimp camarones (m/pl) Kah-Mah-ROON-NeeS

sick enfermo eN-FeRR-MO

sign (display) letrero (m) LeR-TReR-RO

signature firma (f) FeER-Mah

silence silencio See-LeN-See-O

single solo SO-LO

sir señor (m) SeN-YORR

sister hermana (f) eRR-Mah-Nah

size tamaño (m) Tah-Mah-NYO

skin piel (f) PeE-eL

skirt falda (f) Fah-L-Dah

sleeve manga (f) Mah-N-Gah

slowly despacio DeR-SPah-See-O

small pequeño Pe-KeN-YO

smoke (to) fumar FOO-Mah-RR

soap jabón (m) Hah-BON

socks calcetas (f/pl), calcetines (m/pl)
Kah-L-See-TahS, Kah-L-See-TeE-NeeS

some unos (m/pl), unas (f/pl) OO-NOS, OO-NahS
algunos, algunas (w/numbers)
ahL-GOO-NOS, ahL-GOO-NahS

something algo ahL-GO

sometimes algunas veces ahL-Goo-NahS VE-SeS

soon pronto PRON-TO

sorry, I am lo siento LO SEE-eN-TO

soup sopa (f), caldo (m) SO-Pah, KahL-DO

south sur (m) SooR

souvenir recuerdo (m) RE-KWeR-DO

Spanish español (m) eS-PahN-YOL

special especial e-SPe-SEE-ahL

speed velocidad (f) VE-LO-SEE-DahD

spoon cuchara (f) Koo-CHah-Rah

sport deporte (m) De-POR-Te

spring (season) primavera (f) PREE-Mah-VE-Rah

stairs escalera (f) eS-Kah-Le-Rah

stamp sello (m), timbre (m) Se-YO, TeeM-BRe

station estación eS-Tah-SEE-ON

steak bistec (m) BEE-STeK

steamed cocido a vapor KO-SEE-DO ah Vah-POR

stop pare Pah-Re

store tienda (f) TEE-eN-Dah

straight ahead derecho De-Re-CHO

strawberry fresa (f) FRĒ-Sah

street calle (f) Kah-Yē

string cuerda (f) KWĒR-Dah

subway metro (m) MĒ-TRO
   subterráneo (m) (Spain) SooB-Tē-Rah-Nē-O

sugar azúcar (f) ah-Soo-KahR

suit (clothes) traje (m) TRah-Hē

suitcase maleta (f) Mah-Lē-Tah

summer verano (m) Vē-Rah-NO

sun sol (m) SOL

Sunday domingo (m) DO-MĒN-GO

sunglasses lentes de sol (f/pl) LĒN-TēS Dē SOL

suntan lotion loción bronceadora (f)
   LO-Sē-ON BRON-Sē-ah-DOR-ah

supermarket supermercado (m)
   Soo-PēR-MēR-Kah-DO

surprise sorpresa (f) SOR-PRē-Sah

sweet dulce DooL-Sē

swim (to) nadar Nah-DahR

swimming pool piscina (f) PēE-SēE-Nah

synagogue sinagoga (f) SēEN-ah-GO-Gah

T

table mesa (f) ME-Sah

tampons tampones (m/pl) TahM-PO-NES

tape (sticky) cinta (f) SEEN-Tah

tape recorder grabador (m) GRah-Bah-DOR

tax impuesto (m) EEM-PWES-TO

taxi taxi (m) TahK-SEE

tea té (m) TE

telegram telegrama (m) TE-LE-GRah-Mah

telephone teléfono (m) TE-LE-FO-NO

television televisión (f) TE-LE-VEE-SEE-ON

temperature temperatura (f) TEM-PE-Bah-Too-Bah

temple templo (m) TEM-PLO

tennis tenis (m) TE-NEES

tennis court cancha de tenis (f)
    KahN-CHah DE TE-NEES

thank you gracias GRah-SEE-ahS

that ese (m), esa (f) E-SE, E-Sah

the el (m) / la (f) / los (m/pl) / las (f/pl)
    EL / Lah / LOS / LahS

theater teatro (m) TE-ah-TRO

there allí ah-YEE

they ellos (m/pl), ellas (f/pl)   É-YOS,   É-YahS

this este   ÉS-TÉ

thread hilo (m)   ÉE-LO

throat garganta (f)   GahR-GahN-Tah

Thursday jueves (m)   Hoo-É-VÉS

ticket billete (m), boleto (m)
    BÉE-YÉ-TÉ, BO-LÉ-TO

tie corbata (f)   KOR-Bah-Tah

time tiempo (m)   TÉE-ÉM-PO

tip (gratuity) propina (f)   PRO-PÉE-Nah

tire llanta (f)   YahN-Tah

tired cansado   KahN-Sah-DO

toast pan tostado (m)   PahN TO-STah-DO

tobacco tabaco (m)   Tah-Bah-KO

today hoy   OY

together juntos   Hoo N-TOS

toilet baño (m)   Bah N-YO

toilet paper papel higiénico (m)
    Pah-PÉL ÉE-HÉE-ÉN-ÉE-KO

tomato tomate (m)   TO-Mah-TÉ
    jitomate (m)   HÉE-TO-Mah-TÉ

tomorrow mañana   MahN-Yah-Nah

toothache dolor de dientes (m)

　　DO-LOR DE DEE-EN-TES

toothbrush cepillo de dientes (m)

　　SE-PEE-YO DE DEE-EN-TES

toothpaste pasta de dientes (f)

　　PAHS-Tah DE DEE-EN-TES

toothpick palillo (m)　PAH-LEE-YO

tour excursión (f)　EKS-KOOR-SEE-ON

tourist turista (m) (f)　Too-REES-Tah

tourist office oficina de turismo (f)

　　O-FEE-SEE-Nah DE Too-REEZ-MO

towel toalla (f)　TO-ah-Yah

train tren (m)　TREN

travel agent agente de viajes (m)

　　ah-HEN-TE DE VEE-ah-HES

traveler's check cheque de viajero (m)

　　CHE-KE DE VEE-ah-HE-RO

trip viaje (m)　VEE-ah-HE

trousers pantalones (m/pl) PAHN-Tah-LO-NES

trout trucha (f)　TROO-CHah

truth verdad (f)　VER-DahD

Tuesday martes (m)　MAHR-TES

U

umbrella paraguas (m) Pah-Rah-GWahS

understand (to) entender eN-TeN-DeR

underwear ropa interior (f)

ROO-Pah eeN-Te-Ree-OR

United Kingdom Reino Unido RA-NO oo-NEE-DO

United States Estados Unidos (m/pl)

eS-Tah-DOS oo-NEE-DOS

university universidad (f) oo-NEE-VeR-SEE-DahD

up arriba ah-REE-Bah

urgent urgente ooR-HeN-Te

V

vacant desocupado De-SO-Koo-Pah-DO

vacation vacaciones (f/pl) Vah-Kah-SEE-ON-eS

valuable precioso PRe-SEE-O-SO

value valor (m) Vah-LOR

vanilla vainilla (f) VI-NEE-Yah

veal carne de ternera (f) KahR-Ne De TeR-Ne-Rah

vegetables legumbres (f/pl), vegetales (m/pl)

Le-GooM-BReS, Ve-He-Tah-LeS

view vista (f) VEES-Tah

vinegar vinagre (m) VEE-Nah-GRe

voyage viaje (m) VEE-ah-He

W

wait! ¡espérese! ⓔS-Pⓔ-Rⓔ-Sⓔ

waiter camarero (m) Kⓐ-Mⓐ-Rⓔ-Rⓞ
 Spain mozo (m) Mⓞ-THⓞ

waitress camarera (f) Kⓐ-Mⓐ-Rⓔ-Rⓐ
 Spain moza (f) Mⓞ-THⓐ

want, I quiero Kⓔⓔ-ⓔ-Rⓞ

water agua (f) ⓐ-GWⓐ

we nosotros (m/pl) Nⓞ-Sⓞ-TRⓞS

weather tiempo (m) Tⓔⓔ-ⓔM-Pⓞ

Wednesday miércoles (m) Mⓔⓔ-ⓔR-Kⓞ-LⓔS

week semana (f) Sⓔ-Mⓐ-Nⓐ

weekend fin de semana (m)
 FⓔⓔN Dⓔ Sⓔ-Mⓐ-Nⓐ

welcome ¡bienvenido! Bⓔⓔ-ⓔN-Vⓔ-Nⓔⓔ-Dⓞ

well cooked bien cocida Bⓔⓔ-ⓔN Kⓞ-Sⓔⓔ-Dⓐ

west oeste (m) ⓔL ⓞ-ⓔS-Tⓔ

what? ¿qué? Kⓔ / ¿cómo? Kⓞ-Mⓞ

wheelchair silla de ruedas (f)
 Sⓔⓔ-Yⓐ Dⓔ Rⓞⓞ-ⓔ-DⓐS

when? ¿cuándo? KWⓐN-Dⓞ

where? ¿dónde? DⓞN-Dⓔ

which? ¿cuál? KWⓐL

white blanco BLahN-KO

who? ¿quién? KEE-eN

why? ¿por qué? POB-Ke?

wife esposa (f) eS-PO-Sah

window ventana (f) VeN-Tah-Nah

wine list lista de vinos (f) LEES-Tah De VEE-NOS

wine vino (m) VEE-NO

winter invierno (m) eN-VEE-eR-NO

with con KON

woman mujer (f) Moo-HeR

wonderful maravilloso Mah-Rah-VEE-YO-SO

world mundo (m) MooN-DO

wrong equivocado, incorrecto
e-KEE-VO-Kah-DO, eN-KO-BeK-TO

XYZ

year año (m) ahN-YO

yellow amarillo ah-Mah-BEE-YO

yes sí SEE

yesterday ayer ah-YeB

you usted (formal) oo-STeD / tú (informal) Too

zipper cierre (m) SEE-e-Be

zoo zoológico (m) SO-O-LO-HEE-KO

THANKS!

The nicest thing you can say to anyone in any language is "Thank you." Try some of these languages using the incredible EPLS Vowel Symbol System.

Spanish	French
GRah-SEE-ahS	MＥＲ-SEE

German	Italian
Dah'N-Kuh	GRah'T-SEE-ｅ

Japanese	Chinese
DO-MO	SHEEｅ SHEEｅ

Swedish TⓐK	**Portuguese** Ⓞ-BRⒺⒺ-Gⓐ-DⓄ
Arabic SHⓞⓞ-KRⓐN	**Greek** ⓔF-Hⓐ-RⒺⒺ-STⓄ
Hebrew TⓄ-Dⓐ	**Russian** SPⓐ-SⒺⒺ-Bⓐ
Swahili ⓐ-Sⓐ-N-TⒶ	**Dutch** Dⓐ-NK ⓞⓞ
Tagalog Sⓐ-Lⓐ-Mⓐ-T	**Hawaiian** Mⓐ-Hⓐ-LⓄ

INDEX

NOTES

QUICK REFERENCE PAGE

Hello	**Good-bye**
Hola	Adiós
Ō-Lah	ah-DEE-ŌS

How are you?	**Fine / Very well**
¿Cómo está?	Muy bien
KŌ-MŌ ĕS-Tah	MWEE BEE-ĕN

Yes	**No**
Sí	No
SEE	NŌ

Please	**Thank you**
Por favor	Gracias
PŌR Fah-VŌR	GRah-SEE-ahS

I would like...	**Where is...**
Quisiera...	¿Dónde está...
KEE-SEE-ĕ-Rah...	DŌN-Dĕ ĕS-Tah...

I don't understand!

¡No entiendo!

NŌ ĕN-TEE-ĕN-DŌ

Help!

¡Socorro!

SŌ-KŌ-RŌ